# The Monkees,
## Memories and
## the Magic

# The Monkees,
## Memories and the Magic

Edward Wincentsen

[ WP ]

Wynn Publishing

WYNN PUBLISHING
P.O. Box 1491
Pickens, SC 29671

864-878-4328
wynnpub@innova.net

First Printing, March 2000

Copyright 2000 Wynn Publishing

Library of Congress
Catalog Card Number: 00-90204

ISBN: 0-9642808-8-4

All rights reserved. No part of this work may be reproduced or transmitted in whole or part in any form without written permission of the publisher. Brief quotations may be used for the purpose of reviews.

This book is not endorsed or authorized by The Monkees or their representatives. It is solely the work of the author both in research and editing.

Book Design & Layout: Edward Wincentsen

Printed in the USA

# Table of Contents

| | |
|---|---|
| Introduction | 7 |
| The Fans | 12 |
| The Monkees In Concert<br>Sat. January 21, 1967  8:00 p.m. | 109 |
| Alan Green, Davy Jones<br>    and a Book | 121 |
| How To Touch A Monkee | 135 |
| Monkees Good Deeds | 145 |
| Abby Alterio's Story About<br>    a Special Friend | 155 |
| Photo Credits | 166 |
| Credits | 167 |
| Bibliography | 168 |

Dedicated to
Jacquie,
James,
Daniel,
and
Sarah

My family

**The Monkees, Memories and the Magic**

INTRODUCTION

On a Monday evening, September 12, 1966, the first episode of the Monkees T.V. show aired on NBC and life for millions of people would never be the same. That may sound like an exaggeration in numbers, but if you consider all of the first generation fans and later many of their children being fans, plus all the new fans that came with every Monkees revival and anniversary tour, the solo tours, the repeat showings of the original T.V. show on MTV, Nickelodeon and other networks, not to mention the viewersallaround the world, well it all becomes very real indeed!

How did the Monkees and their T.V. show make a change in all these lives? Well, basically it brought us happiness, joy and a escape from whatever troubles and problems we had. There was a lot going on in the world in 1966 and in the years ahead. There was the Vietnam war and it was getting worst. There were friends, sons, cousins, husbands and brothers coming back from the war in coffins. Friends of mine from school were suddenly gone, killed in Vietnam. There was pain, anger and sadness in the country. There was student unrest, the civil rights movement and many other problems. But in the midst of all this was the Monkees. Showing us humor, hope and fun.

The Monkees really did help and in these pages you'll see the proof of that. Sometimes it's easy to just think of the masses of fans as a group of people without separate personalities, but I was forunate enough to be able to look inside and hear the stories and learn the information from them. After all, I was a first generation fan myself. I could relate totally with everyone because I am a part of them and a part of the story too. I am so happy with everyone who helped and contributed to this project and was kind enough to answer my survey questions. I have found that my fellow Monkee fans and friends are some of the most enthusiastic and friendly people around.

This book may seem a little different to the reader. It is not a history of the Monkees, There are not huge sections written about them like a biography, it is not exactly a scrapbook, but you will see them through the words of the fans and some of the stories I have to tell. I would call the various writings 'snapshots' and they do form a complete picture as you progress in the book. I really believe that I have been able to put together something of importance and value here. My goal has been to show how the Monkees have brought joy and happiness to millions of people. The material I have from the fans only represents a small portion, but you could say it's an indicator of what other stories are out there. Maybe from my humble work we will all think more when we talk to a new, fellow Monkee fan. Maybe we will have more compassion and love. I also wanted to show people who are not Monkees fans what all the fuss is about and why we care. If this book accomplishes these things I will be most grateful.

Also, the same could be said about my 'Monkee Good Deed' section. There are, of course, many, many more stories about each of the guys, but I just didn't have access to them. Again, hopefully these few stories will be an indicator of what other stories are out there. This book starts out with stories and information from the fans of every generation. Then there are other stories about experiences with the Monkees as a group and as individuals. There's a little of everything for everybody. It's memories, as the title suggests, but it is also the magic of the Monkees that I think you will see shining through. Since the book starts with the fans memories and experiences I think this would be a good place to tell the reader a little about myself and how I became a Monkees fan.

I had graduated from high school and started classes at a college, but I dropped out. Since the Vietnam war was going on I knew it would only be a matter of time before I was drafted into the Army so I thought it would be better to be in the Navy than be a foot soldier. I enlisted and almost right away I had problems. I got a very bad case of pneumonia in boot camp and was transferred to the Balboa Navel Hospital in San Diego right across from the Balboa Zoo. Later as I was put back into active duty I was sent to Communications Yeoman School in Norfolk, Virginia. This was right in the middle of their winter and I had a relapse of the pneumonia. This also started up again my childhood asthma. I received a discharge from the Navy and went back home to Phoenix, Arizona hurting very badly and feeling quite useless and depressed.

My spirits were at an all time low. I wondered how I could work, or hold a job. I had to lay down on my bed several hours each day to try to heal and build up my strength. Then my mother, God Bless her soul, encouraged me and told me that I could work if I found a job that wasn't physical. I went through a private employment agency and got a job as a clerk at a bank. It wasn't easy, but I was making it through the day even though I had to still rest in my bed after I got home. That's when I heard 'Last Train to Clarksville' on the radio. I liked the song and I liked the sound of the guitar. The DJ said that this was the Monkees and they would be on a T.V. series starting on September 12th on a Monday night. I made a mental note to watch it. After all, Monday night was pretty easy to remember. Well, the day came and I watched the show and I was hooked. I wasn't going to miss any of those shows from now on I said to myself. I was slowly getting better and gaining my strength. My job was going good and I enjoyed the people at work.

The Monkees T.V. show cheered me up, it made me laugh and I started to think that there was still hope and happiness and fun in the world and I wanted to be a part of it. I got the Monkees first album and loved it. It went right with all my Beatles albums and all the other music of the day. I was a big music fan and the sixties were really happening as far as music went. But the Monkees, along with their T.V. show, seemed to hold a special place in my heart. They helped me heal and have hope and joy again. Later, in this book, I will relate the story of seeing the Monkees concert in Phoenix, Arizona in 1967. By doing this book and connecting with others in the Monkees network I found another fan who was at that same concert as me. Boy, that's amazing when I think about it, and a great joy! These days of computers are really something! The Phoenix, Arizona concert was captured on film for the Monkees T.V. episode entitled 'Monkees on Tour' which was the last episode of the first season. It also has clips of the guys at various places in Phoenix.

Well, enjoy the pages that are ahead. In 'The Fans' section if one story does not interest you, just skip over it. I guarantee you'll find stories that are interesting and very moving. Maybe they will even rekindle some of your own Monkees memories.

## The Fans

Monkees fans come in all shapes and sizes and ages and can be found in almost every walk of life. Caroline Walsh is a writer with The Irish Times and wrote this article that I am using excerpts of. The article which was entitled 'I Was A Monkees Fan In The 1960s' was published January 21, 1997 to announce a concert that the Monkees were to do in Dublin (Used by permission). The article is quite interesting.

"Hey, hey, what the hell. Some secrets get too hot to handle. Maybe it's bye-bye to many friends and colleagues I value highly but it's true I was a Monkees fan in the 1960s.

Set to roll into Dublin to play at the Point on March 10th. It'as all part of a nine-venue tour of Britain and Ireland that will culminate in the 12,000-seat Wembley Arena a few days later.

The last time I thought about these guys I was a 14-year-old with poor skin – can't bear to say acne – and black-rimmed, Dame-Edna-style glasses, recently transplanted from an all-girl Irish secondary school to a New England high school every bit as zappy as Degrassi High. While half the world my age was turning on, tuning in and dropping out, I was sitting in front of the TV set cravenly singing along to 'I'm a Believer.'

The Monkees phenomenon was apparently dreamed up by TV channel executives to provide clean, all-American TV and lyrics for a generation that had suddenly begun to wear its hair long, run around in open-toe sandals, refuse to go to war and started smoking some weedy kind of thing that could lead to worse. Understandably, parents loved the Monkees.

Within five minutes of arriving in the US for that first time, I'd bought Barry McGuire's album 'Eve of Destruction,' got hold of a black maxi coat and was driving my mother crazy talking about heading out to Haight-Ashbury. Still it was hard not to sing along when the Monkees came on screen sing 'Last Train To Clarksville.'

Micky Dolenz was definitely the sexy one. Davy Jones was the one all the American girls wanted but even then, were we to have come face to face, I knew I'd be taller than him (he'd been a jockey in another life). Coming from Ireland, he being a Mancunian didn't have for me the cachet it seemed to have for all those blonde Connecticut girls I was in school with; they were in awe of him, I was in awe of them.

Mike Nesmith might have been more attractive if he'd taken off that woolly hat; anyway he was always the serious one.

Then there's the survivor syndrome. The sheer admiration for the fact that they've come through life's trials and tribulations. Davy Jones jokes that the money made from the reunion will come in handy for alimony. Peter Tork talks about the bumps on the road but, hell, they're still prepared to get up on stage and shake a leg.

To me it's all tied up with that time of high adolescence as a sophomore at E.O. Smith High School where, within hours of being parachuted into its gleaming corridors thronged with confident teenagers. I'd made a friend in Chris Thorkelson: lots of hair, steel-rimmed glasses – and the kid brother of Peter Tork.

At the outset it has to be said that in spite of visits to the Thorkelson home I never met the mop-haired Pete which I was sorry about then and, reading about him now, am sorry about still. He sounds an interesting guy: those years he put in prior to the Monkees, hanging around Greenwich Village, playing in a folk group with Stephen Stills and all those things he has to say now about the difference between the grunge and alternative music of today and the folk songs of 30 years ago. He says they had room to believe in love then, today "it's all angst."

*

The material next was complied and written by Susan A. Santo and entitled 'Why We Loved The Monkees, Experiences of First Generation Fans.' I am just using excerpts of special interest, but if the reader would like to read it in it's entirety just go to www.monkees.net/monkees/docs/survey.htm Susan wrote, "The results (her survey, done in the 80's) show that far from being a shallow attachment that soon faded, their (the fans) love for the Monkees had a profound effect on their lives." This is exactly the point I'm making in this book as well. The reader can see if they can identify with any of the statements by these fans."The first thing that endeared them to me was their smiles. I felt loved by them."

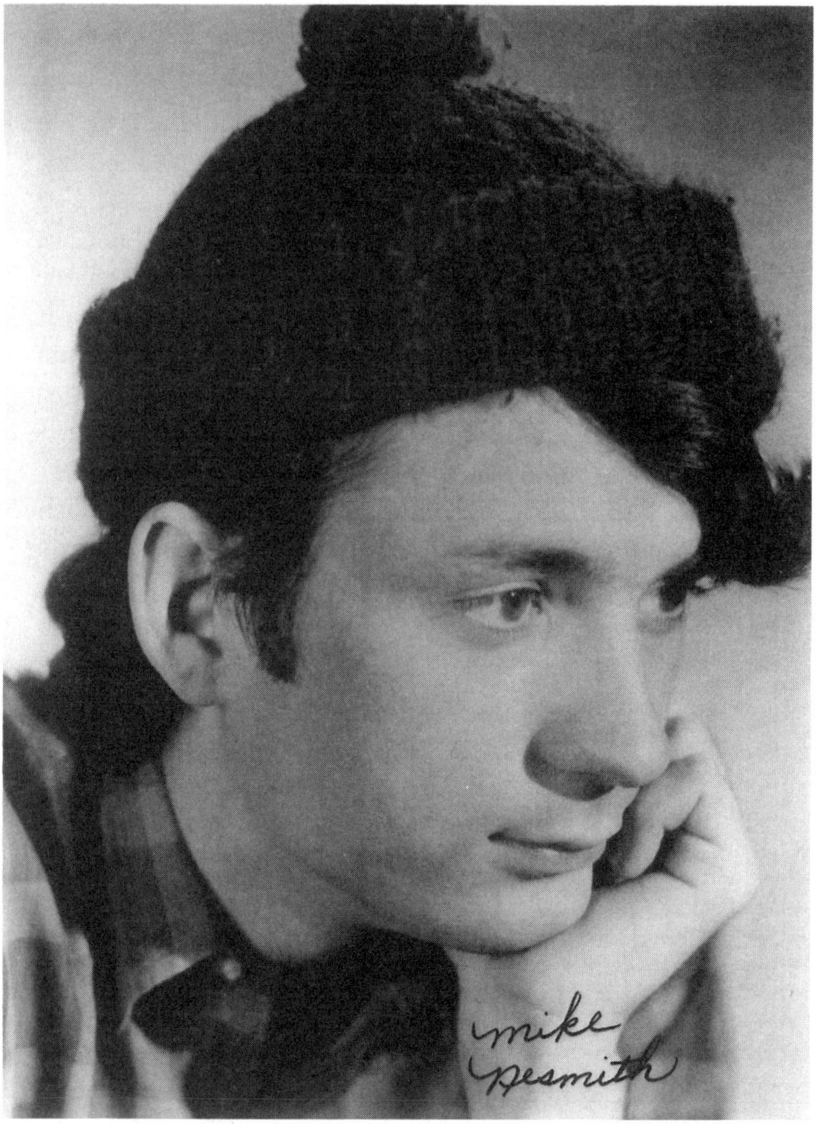
mike
nesmith

"I had a pretty unhappy, lonely time of it through much of my teenage years. The Monkees were an escape. My parents thought it was ridiculous and that I should try to get a real boyfriend instead of dreaming about Davy Jones all the time. But when you're 14 years old, the boys in your class are not as mature as the girls. We girls wanted romance, we wanted to fall in love. But the boys were creeps; they were either still at the stage where they pulled the girl's hair, or else they'd take you out and the date would turn into a wrestling match. So that's where the Monkees fit in. These guys were perfect to dream about! They never disappointed us, they didn't let us down. The magazines assured us that our favorite teen idols were kind, considerate, romantic, everything we wanted them to be. I remember looking forward to the next issue of 'Monkee Spectacular' with such eagerness and poring over each article. And as corny as those fan magazines were, they helped us kids. My friends and I wanted to be the kind of girls that the Monkees would like, so we followed the advice of these magazines not to take drugs or smoke or whatever."

"It was Micky right from the start. I loved his humor, his cute little face, his singing, and most of all his adorable shyness. I was off in my own world a lot. In that world, I was Micky's best friend and we could talk about everything. He was a favorite companion to a very lonely child."

"Something adults didn't understand – apparently, even Peter (Tork) himself didn't – was that to kids, Peter wasn't dumb at all; he was a child in spirit: innocent, loving, giving, unspoiled by bad experiences. Perhaps we hoped that if Peter could do it, we'd be able to hang on to what was good in us, too."

"During the Sixties with the Vietnam war and all the

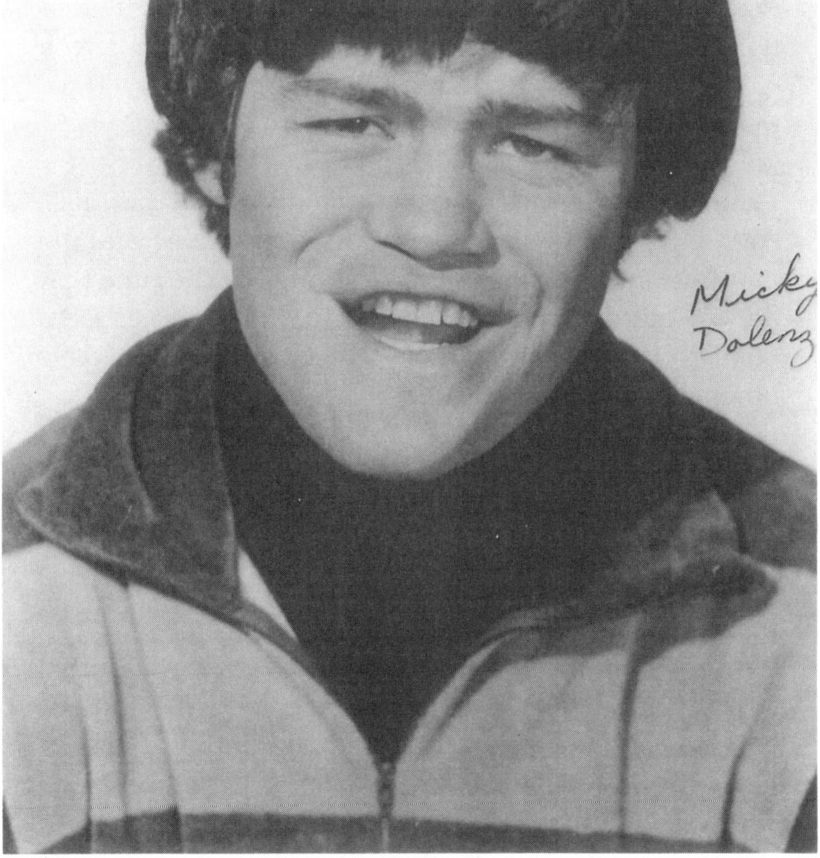
Micky
Dolenz

rebellion I think the Monkees were a bit of an escape for me. I was not ready to face all that conflict. Burying myself in them I did not have to see the campus protests and killing on the TV, and I did not have to think too much about my brother being in Vietnam, the memorial services for the boys who had just graduated the year before. That was a pretty scary time; did the Monkees keep us sane?"

"I cried bitterly when the show ended, when Peter left. I tried to understand. I still bought all the records and saw them in reruns. I felt alone and I missed them. I never stopped loving them. It left a gap. I kept it to myself and wondered and prayed for them always. They were a part of me."

"The Sixties, which had begun with such promise, ended in hatred with violent riots, drug abuse, and the dissolution of the 'Love Generation.' By the time that decade of love had come to an end, the Monkees were gone too. It seemed they were a product of their times, destined not to outlast it. Or were they?"

*

Here's a poignant and moving account of what Monkee fan Miki, from Ferndale, Michigan, had to share. It also shows the magic of the Monkees. "I'm now 25, I've been a fan of the Monkees for about 20 years. I saw their TV show when I was little and got hooked. When I was younger I had a lot of trouble in school because I had severe dysxlia. It took forever for me to be able to read a book. I didn't go near books unless it was for the pictures. I could draw better than my teachers when I was in the 7th grade. I got ahold of a copy of Davy's book 'They Made A Monkee Out of Me' and that was the first book I ever sat thru and read. It took me a long time to make it through it, but I was determined to read it. I was in the 6th grade at

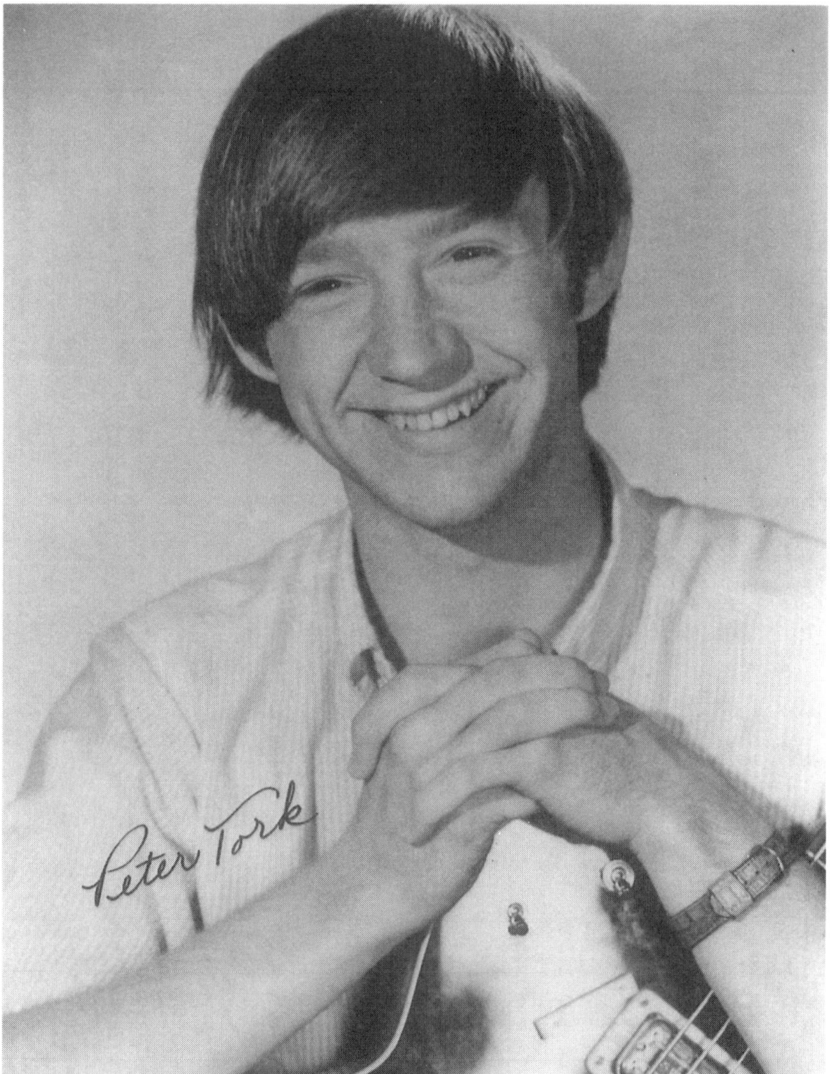
Peter Tork

**DAVID JONES**

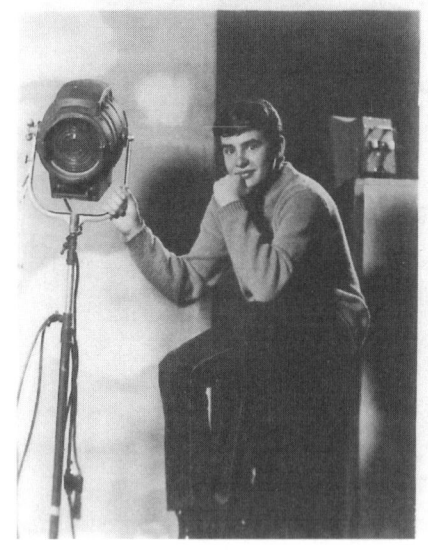

Early Davy Jones

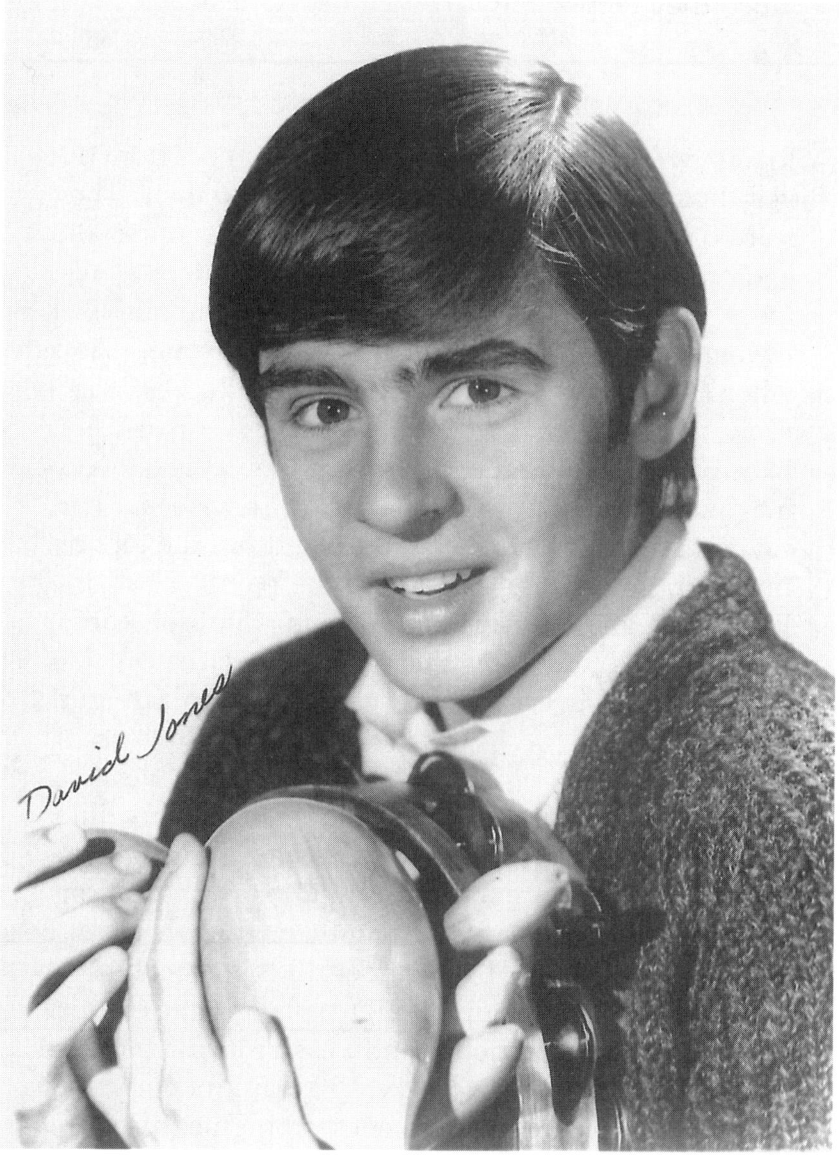
David Jones

the time. I about taught myself to read finishing that book. I then read 'Who's Got the Button' and old magazines that I got ahold of. They have no idea how much they helped me."

*

Joanna wrote this, "I have loved the Monkees from the very beginning, 1966. I was nine years old then. They started showing the commercials for the show at the end of the summer and it captivated my interest. Yes, I was there, Monday September 12, 7:30 pm on NBC. I was hooked from the opening theme song. And when I saw Davy Jones' face that was it !!!

I bought every album up to 'Instant Replay' andevery magazine that had their faces on it. I wished I had saved them, but I cut them all up and put the pics on my wall, you couldn't even see the paint. I had the lunch box and was in the fan club. Trading cards, comic books, anything that had their faces on it, I wanted. And everywhere I went, my Monkees stuff went, too.

As far as what was going on in my life at this time, well, I was a kid growing up in the suburbs during the 60's. I had the normal bumps and bruises, triumphs and tragedies that everyone had then. But whenever I hear Monkee songs, I remember all the good times I had as a kid. Sitting up all night, playing the albums over and over. My friends and I each playing the part of our favorite Monkee (if I wasn't Davy, nobody was playing) and acting out scenes from the show, or maybe a romp. I even took music lessons in school so I could learn to play Monkee songs – you haven't lived till you've heard 'Steppin' Stone' played on a clarinet."

*

Davy Jones

Charlyne, who shared some of her Monkees photo collection for this book, had this to say, "I first became aware of the Monkees in 1966, both by TV and the radio. I was 10 years old at the time. Previously, I had liked the Beatles, but by 1966 they had become a little too 'weird' for me. Being raised in a conservative home, I found the Monkees to be more down to earth and normal for my liking. To be honest, I really don't remember seeing the Monkees debut on TV, but I do remember watching the show during it's initial run. Although I liked the Monkees as a whole, I did have a favorite 'Monkee' that I related to and he was Peter. The reason I related to him was that as I was growing up in grade school I was picked on because I was a small person. I felt sorry for Peter because he was always picked on in the TV show. I could relate to him as I was treated the same way and felt a 'bond' with him. Back then, in my 10 year old mind I felt that the Monkees were real. That their characters they played on theTV show were their real selves. As I grew older, I then knew that the Monkees were just actors on the TV show, but the 'bond' with Peter remained.

I never was able to go to a Monkees concert back then because of my age. However, in 1967 I was able to meet one of the Monkees. On January 1, 1967 the Monkees were in concert in Nashville, TN. I lived in Nashville and on that particular day my parents and I were downtown. Somehow, my dad got the word that the Monkees were staying at a motel called the "own-towner"and he took me over there in the chance that I might see them. As we got to the motel, who do I see but Micky standing in the parking lot! And amazingly, there weren" many people around! My dad encouraged me to go up to Micky and get his autograph. I found a scrap piece of paper for Micky to sign. I was so nervous and extremely shy, but I did manage to go up to Micky and he signed the paper. Immediately following this, I remember looking up at

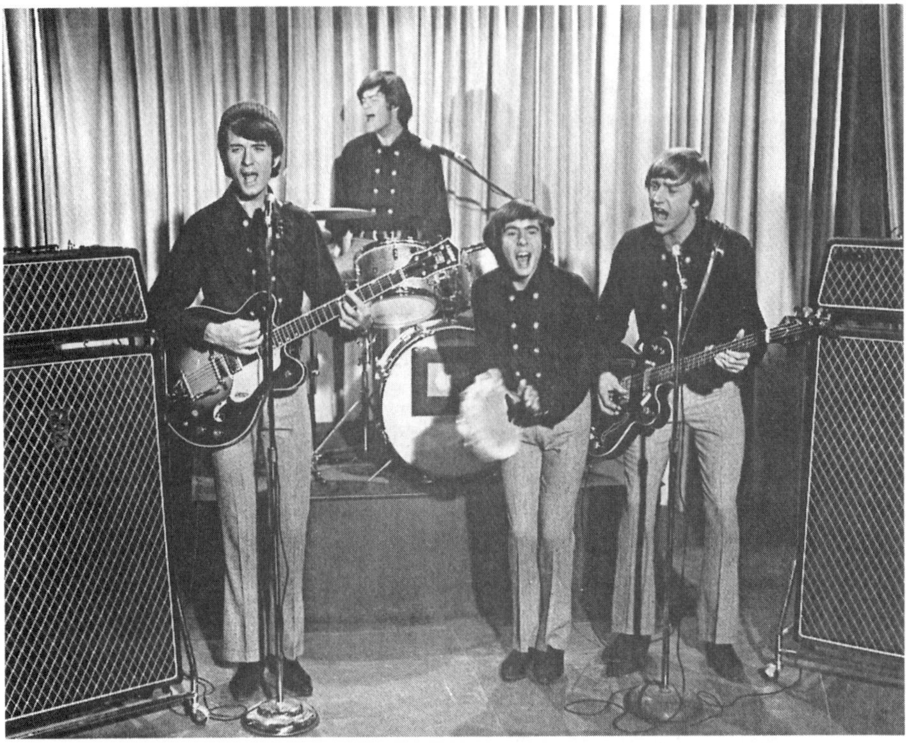

the motel and saw Mike standing on the third or fourth floor balcony which overlooked the parking lot. I'll always have fond memories of seeing Micky and Mike that day in 1967."

*

Here's a fan from England, Lyn, and she writes, "I first saw the Monkees on U.K. Television on New Years Eve, 1966. Also, on the radio. They made me feel happy, made me wish I could live on the same beach with them. And they also made me wish I was a little older than the 12 years I was at the time. I was a secondary school pupil (high school) living at home with my mother and two younger siblings. My father had left some years before, and it was a struggle for my mother to make ends meet. But, she always found the money to be able to buy the singles, albums, Monthlies and Annuals too. U.K. pop music was at it's very best, but for me the Monkees were the tops.

Perhaps I have been living in a fantasy world all these years, but it doesn't seem to have done me any harm! The TV series was escapism for me. I loved it."

*

Here's some more of the magic of the Monkees and what they could do, and still do. A fan by the name of Destiny wrote, "I first learned of the Monkees when my mother was watching the Disney Channel and there was a documentary of the Monkees on it. My mother made me watch the program. She wanted me to see what she use to watch when she was little. At first I had no interest in it, and I made fun of the Monkees, but then I saw the 'Randy Scouse Git' video and fell in love with Micky, because he really made me laugh. I have been a hard core fan ever since."

Davy and Peter

When asked what was going on in her life when she first discovered the Monkees Destiny replied, "To tell you the truth…a lot. I can not explain what though because it's too personal and I don't wish to share it, but I can this with my whole heart and soul….the Monkees really helped me get through it. I honestly think that's why I love them so much. As corny as it may sound, it's the truth. They also introduced the art of music to my life as well. I now have a passion for playing music, and maybe even make a career out of it someday too. All this is credited to the Monkees. I have now met Davy. He's a real sweetheart. I found him to be one of the nicest men that I've ever met."

*

Here is another account that shows the magic of what the Monkees could do for their fans. Michele wrote, "I first became aware of the Monkees in 1973 when I was just 6 years old. At that point in my life the Monkees were just a bunch of cool, goofy guys who sang. I saw their television show on our local station during the weekdays after school when I was 9. I was happy and couldn't wait to get home from school to watch the show. I really didn't realize that the Monkees themselves were a music group until I was in my teens and started collecting their original albums, but they were like friends that you can't wait to see and are sorry to see leave.

At that time my mother and father were just going through a nasty divorce and we spent a lot of time moving around the state. The Monkees were a stability in my life, something I could always count on being there. Whenever I was upset I would go into my room and play my records and I'd remember the romp scenes that went with that particular song and it always made me feel better."

Davy and Mike

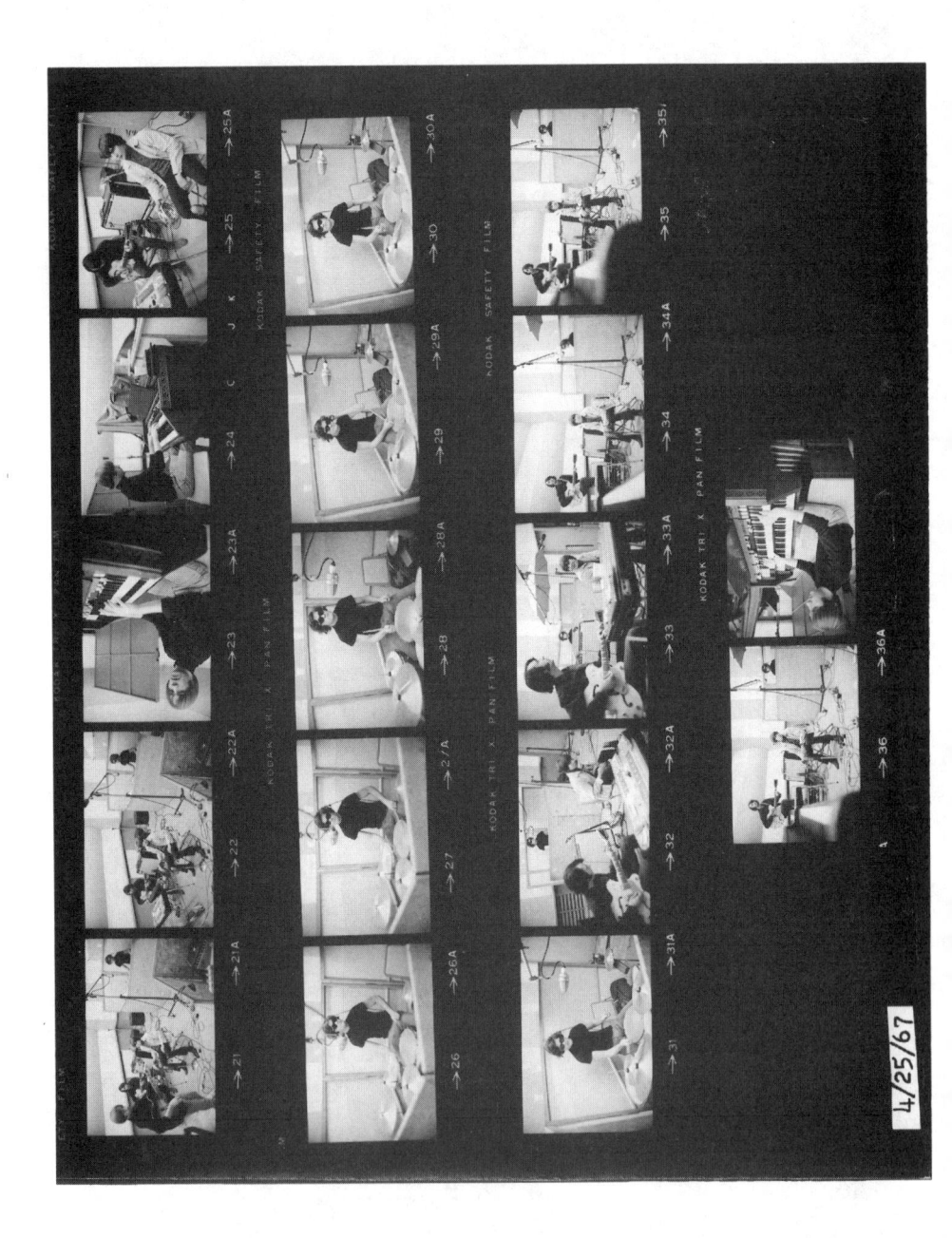

Monkees early recording session

4/25/67

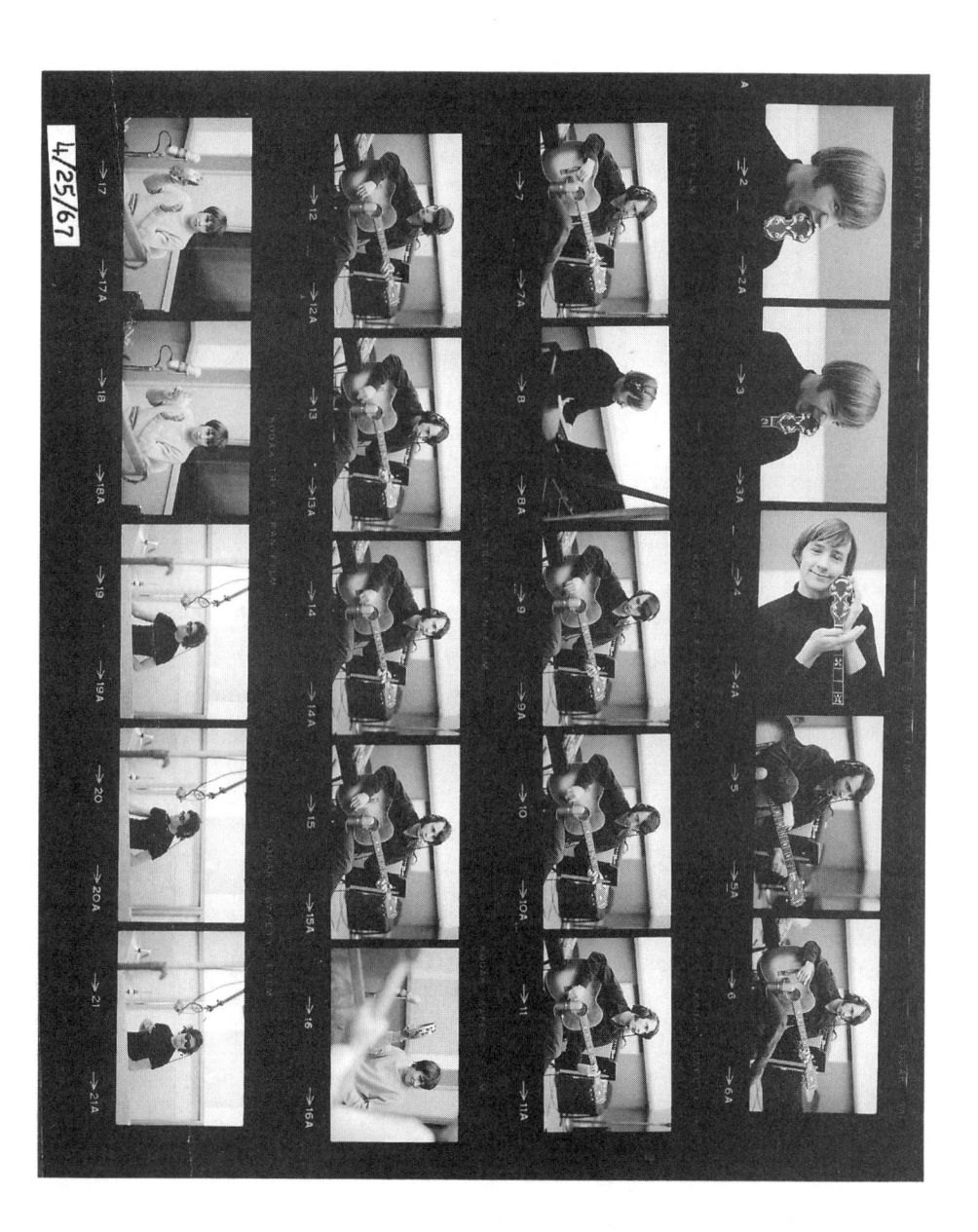

\*

Here's some feedback from a German fan, Birgit, and how the Monkees helped her in learning English. "Being a Monkees addict living in Berlin, Germany is not the most common thing. I've been a fan since 1988 when sky television aired the show around Europe via satellite. I was 12 years old at the time and immediately fell for them, though I only understood about half of what was said because I was just starting to learn English. So you could say that the Monkees helped me a lot to improve my English! I always had to walk over to my grandmother's then because she had a TV set which could receive the right channel. I watched the Monkees along with 'I Dream of Jeannie,' 'Get Smart,' and 'Three's Company,' but all I really cared about was them, which kind of left me standing alone. I had only two friends who marginally understood what I was all about. One came from the US, so she understood the show. The other was a sixties fan and really did her best to be a fan, though she always liked the Beatles better.

I went on about them for about three years until I decided I was too old for that, and neglected them until this year. It all started again when I surfed the InterNet sites about the guys just for fun, and suddenly I couldn't understand what had made me ignore them for this long. I started watching my videos again and to establish mail contact with other US fans."

\*

Theresa lives with her husband in Gainesville, GA on Lake Lanier, and in a cabin too. Boy, what a life! Anyway, here's what Theresa had to share. "I'm a first generation fan. I was 9 years old at the time the show first came on. The TV show was what first introduced me to the Monkees, but since the song 'The Last Train to Clarksville' came out over the radio first I might have heard that before the TV show. I literally ate-slept-breathed Monkees. Of course in addition to all the albums, I had all the merchandise as well. I can still recall how goofy I looked in that wool hat! I never saved my Monkees stuff so I'm doing my best to retrieve it all back."

*

Cindy had this to say, "I first became aware of the Monkees in 1966 through the Teen Magazines before the TV series started. The Monkees affected me...oh, I was 12 years old. Of course I fell in love with them !!! As far as what was going on in my life then, I was 12, what wasn't going on in my life? It was 1966 and I was just becoming socially aware of the world, boys, music, etc. I was learning to draw and paint. I would spend hours in my room listening to the radio and using teen magazine pinups to learn to draw. The very first water color portrait I did was of David. I saved it and 25 years later I gave it to him. When I hear 'Daydream Believer' on the radio it takes me back to that room and the hours I spent painting – it is a wonderful, warm memory. It was the best time of my life.

The Monkees were and are something very special. I doubt that anyone can put it into words that would make someone who doesn't understand, understand. It's like the 60's – you had to be there. There are so many dynamics involved. It was the time, it was our age, it was the music, it was the comedy, it was their chemistry, it was the way they were marketed. Some things were not meant to be explained. They tried to duplicate it in the 80's and couldn't because the Monkees were unique. There are only 4 guys who will ever be the Monkees and there is a bond that keeps us all together. Maybe we shouldn't spend so much time trying to figure it out and just enjoy it.

My biggest saddness is that there is nothing to compare today and that the kids growing up today lose their innocence much too quickly – never knowing what it is like to be totally carefree and believe completely that there are 4 lads living in a beach house in California making music and falling in love 10 times a day, and having a song like 'Daydream Believer,' sweet and simple to play in the soundtrack of their lives."

*

Here is material from Lisa of Brown University. "I'm a second generation fan. I first became aware of the Monkees in the spring of 1975 when the show went into national syndication on local TV stations. I was 9 years old at the time. I've been a Monkees fan for 24 years, since I was 9 years old. I think it's had a major effect on my life, and that it's been a positive thing. I've made a lot of good friends out of the Monkees experience. There are some people I just see at concerts and collectible shows and that's it. But there are other people that have become some of my best friends. I think there's more to the relationships that are long lasting than a common interest in the Monkees; that's a great starting point but you need something more to sustain a 10 year relationship. But I wouldn't have met these folks without that common starting point.

My interest in the Monkees have also given me a hobby that I still enjoy, collecting records and Monkees memorabilia.

I was an elementary school student when I first became aware of the Monkees. Nothing special was going on – I was a good student and I had a core

Davy and Micky in the studio

group of friends. A few years later I had a tough time at school due to other kids teasing me, rather nastily (although I always had some good friends). This teasing was not related to my liking the Monkees, those people didn't know about that. Because I was an honors student with a heavy course-load and because of the rough time I was having with the teasing it was nice to have a fun hobby (watching the Monkees and listening to their music and collecting) as a pressure release when I came home."

\*

Vanessa writes, "I first became aware of the Monkees when I was about the age of 4. I watched them on Saturday mornings around 1978. Then when I was 12 I really fell in love with them and have been hooked ever since. The Monkees have had a huge effect on my life. So much so that my sister-in-law and I run a Monkees fan club called HeadQuarters. We have done the fan club for 5 years now. They have showed me that I don't have to be serious all the time and that laughter is the best medicine. When I first discovered the Monkees I was in the 6th grade and lots of stuff was going on. Being a girl it was the typical, "am I pretty? do the boys like me?" kind of stuff, but mostly it was just a time when my best friend and I could daydream about marrying Davy and Micky."

You can check out Vanessa's club at: www.geocities.com/TelevisionCity/Studio/2173 and it is now an official authorized club by Davy Jones.

\*

Mary had this to say, "I first became aware of the Monkees around 1985, I was born in 1979. I discovered them through the TV show and I loved them !!!! And still do. My friends and I used to pretend to be

The Monkees arriving in Australia

the Monkees. I was usually Micky because I looked the most like him (even though I'm a girl). Micky is my favorite. I was then in second grade. At that point I was learning to write and probably chasing boys, or something. The TV show was only on for awhile when I was little, but it made a big enough impression on me to remember them! Then, over two years ago, I became the ultimate Monkees Freak. I know all their songs, have all of the TV episodes and tape all of their appearances on TV."

*

Debbie, from England, had some interesting and inspirational information to share, "I first became aware of David Jones in 1962. I was 9 years old at the time and he was appearing in an episode of 'Z Cars' which was an early soap opera about life in the police force. David played a child shoplifter. He stole some sweets and was caught by the shopkeeper who called the police. I can stillremember begging my mother to find out his name and where he came from. I saw him again sometime later in another soap called 'Coronation Street' where he played Ena Sharple's grandson. After that he disappeared as far as I knew, and although I wrote to several agencies and TV companies, I was never able to find out why, or where he had gone. Then, one dreary day at school some friends were talking about the great show they had seen on TV and how dreamy the guys were. I asked them what it was and they persuaded me to watch the following show. Well, I nearly fell off the chair when the titles came up. I shouted to my mother to come and see who was on TV and she recognised David straight away.

The effect the Monkees had on me was profound. I am a true first generation fan. The show quickly became the focus of my week, I literally could not wait for Saturday (the show was a different day and time in

Davy

England) to come around and if I was required to go out with my parents well, I would just make a fuss and sulk until they said I could stay home !!! I religiously purchased Monkees Monthly and also joined the fan club in America. I was 14 at the time and studying for my first exams at school. I would try and do this in my room, but the walls were full of pictures of David and I often got distracted! My father realized that it was not just an infatuation on my part and that I really admired David's talent. No more so than when he encouraged me to become the President of David's English fan club, which I ran successfully for 3 years after I was diagnosed with multiple sclerosis. After that time I became too unwell to manage the club. It was, however, thinking of David's own determination and zest for life that convinced me to go ahead and open the club."

*

Frances from Wales, United Kingdom wrote, "I am a member of the Monkees UK fan club 'Band 6.' I have been a fan since 1967 and saw them at one of their first UK concerts at Wembley, England in that year. I have finally met each of the Monkees! They have been a big presence in my life, both then and now."

*

Here's a very touching and emotional account by Kelly in Virginia, "I first became aware of the Monkees in 1985, I was 8 years old. I saw Davy Jones on 'The Brady Bunch' and asked my mother who he was. Then anytime a Monkees song came on the radio after that, she would point it out, and I always liked what I heard. When I was 8 years old I had just revealed to my parents my secret of having been molested at age 4, we were having a lot of family problems and our 15 year old cocker spaniel had just

Peter & Mike in the movie, 'Head.'

died.

The Monkees were my comic relief when MTV started airing the episodes in the 80's. Their music was my hiding place. They were my friends when no one else was, and they made me feel less alone. They were silly, and fun, and happy…..they made me feel that way, too.

I am one of the biggest Monkee fans out there, and I can tell you that I have followed their tours everywhere! The furthest I have gone is when I followed them to Scotland, during the UK tour in 1997 because Mike was touring with them and I simply had to see them perform together at least once in my life."

\*

Sandy Mearing shared this, "I am a 40 year old mom of two children. They are also fans, as of the recent 30th anniversery. I first became aware of the Monkees in 1966 through the television show. I was only 7 at the time. When I saw the show, seen the guys and heard the music I knew they were something special. I never missed the show. I was not the typical 7 year old, I didn't play kids games much, I preferred to listen to music, watch TV and read teen idol magazines. I think I acted more like a teenager than a 7 year old. When I found the show that was all it took and I was devoted. The show was funny, fresh, creative, fun, and the music was excellent. All four guys were great and had their own appeal, and good looks. The chemistry of the guys was perfect, no one else could have done it then, and I don't think anyone else could do it today. It was a once-in-a-lifetime thing.

I have been enjoying buying things off ebay that I didn't previously have in my collection, making cyber friends via email with other Monkees fans, and surfing all the great websites."

*

Here's an example of 1st and 2nd generation fans, both in the same family. Tiffany wrote, "I first became aware of the Monkees in 1998 when I was 12 years old. I was on a whole 60's kick and was searching the house for anything from that decade. I found a couple TV episodes of the Monkees and a cd of my mom's lying around, and I was hooked. I was talking to my mom one night about my latest interests and when I mentioned the Monkees she got really excited. It turned out that when she was about my age, she too was a fan and her favorite Monkee was the same as mine, Micky. She told me about how she got to meet him in a hotel lobby in Miami in 1967. I've gotten to see Davy in concert twice since then (both with the Teen Idols Tour) and Micky once (also with the Teen Idol Tour)."

*

Sharon from Easley, South Carolina had this to share about growing up with the Monkees, "I first became aware of the Monkees from their TV show in 1966. I was only 10 years old at the time so it was just the usual day to day stuff going on in my life at that time. One of my earliest recollections of the Monkees is when I first heard them on the radio singing 'Last Train to Clarksville.' I begged my mom for that 45. It was the first record I got (that wasn't Walt Disney stuff). I had always wanted a Monkees lunchbox, but never got it. Now I have one along with a good collection of Monkees memorabilia. My kids and husband don't think I'll ever grow up! I used to tape every TV show on my reel to reel tape recorder. I wouldn't let anyone in the house talk while I was recording the show. Everyone had to tiptoe around."

Dawn Lively (what a nice name) shared this, "I first became aware of the Monkees sometime in the mid 70's. I had always, at that age (about 4 or 5), thought that I was '1st generation' because they were on every afternoon at 12:30 on a channel out of Chicago, and at that age I wasn't really aware of the concept of reruns. I watched the show every day whenever I got the chance. It was just understood that the TV was mine at that time. I don't really remember them much on the radio, but that's probably because I wasn't around when they were actually big. Being that young at the time, I don't recall specifically why I was so.....not obsessed, but very interested in them. I always liked their music. They were pretty funny too. The Monkees made me one of those weirdos that would mention them from time to time before they made their MTV comeback in the 80's.

I remember my cousin and I trying to stay up all night to record all of the Monkees episodes on tape when MTV ran their Monkees Marathon while we were in high school (80's). Unfortuantely we missed some of the shows towards the end. Not many shows like that anymore."

*

Here's comments from Daniel, down under in Australia, "I became aware of the Monkees in 1967, at the age of 9. I lived in Hawthorn east, Melbourne Victoria, Australia. I went to Auburn South State school and a school friend told me about the Monkees being on TV. At first I didn't know what he was talking about and went to his home to watch the show because he lived nearby. I remember the episode being that of the pilot episode because I distinctly remember the bar room scene where the Monkees are

Davy in the stageplay, 'Godspell.'

wearing masks running, with the bartender watching. At the time I couldn't understand the show because it was so new and innovative....I needed to see more episodes, then I became a fan. I'm 42 years old and I have a fantastic Monkees collection and I'm still a great Monkees fan. The Monkees music was my introduction to pop/country because of the great songs by Michael Nesmith."

*

Another fan writes, "I was a 5th grader, just shy of 10 years old when I discovered the Monkees in September 1966. The kids on my school bus were singing their songs and passing around pictures from teen magazines with their pictures in it. The Monkees have endured all these years, and 33 years later I still listen to their albums, and get a warm, fuzzy feeling when their songs come on the radio."

*

Cassie Sparks, from Southwest Virginia, must have been the youngest fan ever. She had this to share, "I first became aware of the Monkees in 1987 when I was 2 years old. I was watching this tv show with a lot of music and just started watching the guys. I fell in love with Davy, who I knew as the 'short guy' back then. Later, I sort of forgot about them through the years, until 1997 when they were in Kingsport, TN. My parents and I went to see them. So I became aware of them again at the concert.

Well, when I learned of them it was like....Wow! They're great singers...and such cute, loveable, funny guys....and I was constantly wanting to meet them....especially Davy and Peter. That was in 1997, but in 1987 it was, 'Mommy, I wanna watch the Monkees.' Their music is still kind of new to me. I

The Monkees bubblegum cards

find new songs by them all the time."

*

Sarah wrote, "I became a Monkees fan in mid 1997 when I saw their TV show on Nick at Nite. I saw an advertisement about the show and thought that it would be a cool show, so I watched it. I really liked it, but then Nick at Nite took it off the air. I totally fell in love with Davy, and since then I have been collecting all kinds of Monkees stuff like records, dolls, pictures, lunch boxes, cards and anything else I can get my hands on. I like Davy because I think he's a really sweet guy and he cares about his fans."

*

Bob in Mineola, New York gives a male perspective, "Being born in 1962 meant that I was very young when the first phenomenon of both the Beatles and the Monkees took place. However, enjoying music and cartoons had an effect on me. When the Beatles cartoons surfaced, this became a vehicle for me to enjoy their music, all the while being a cartoon watching kid. At that time my folks had a black and white TV, so when I watched the Monkees for content. I always enjoyed the 'romp' scenes, and the bizarre camera angles! Parents didn't understand this, and it became something for the kids only! So, I knew of the Monkees when they were originally aired, but I became most aware of them during their Saturday run in 1970.

In regards to school I always thought of having my friends be a group of guys that were singers, or just sharing a place, or acting silly, like the Monkees' romps would be. I do remember looking for a blue wool hat, and I wore it through the school halls (in the 1970's!) as I wanted to be Mike! A friend from school

L. to R. Alan Green, Davy Jones & the author at Alan's house.

Micky in a dress, with Peter.

Davy in action.

My color design of Davy that appeared in Davy's book, 'Mutant Monkees.'

52

Another color design of mine of Davy & Dudley Moore that did not appear in 'Mutant Monkees.'

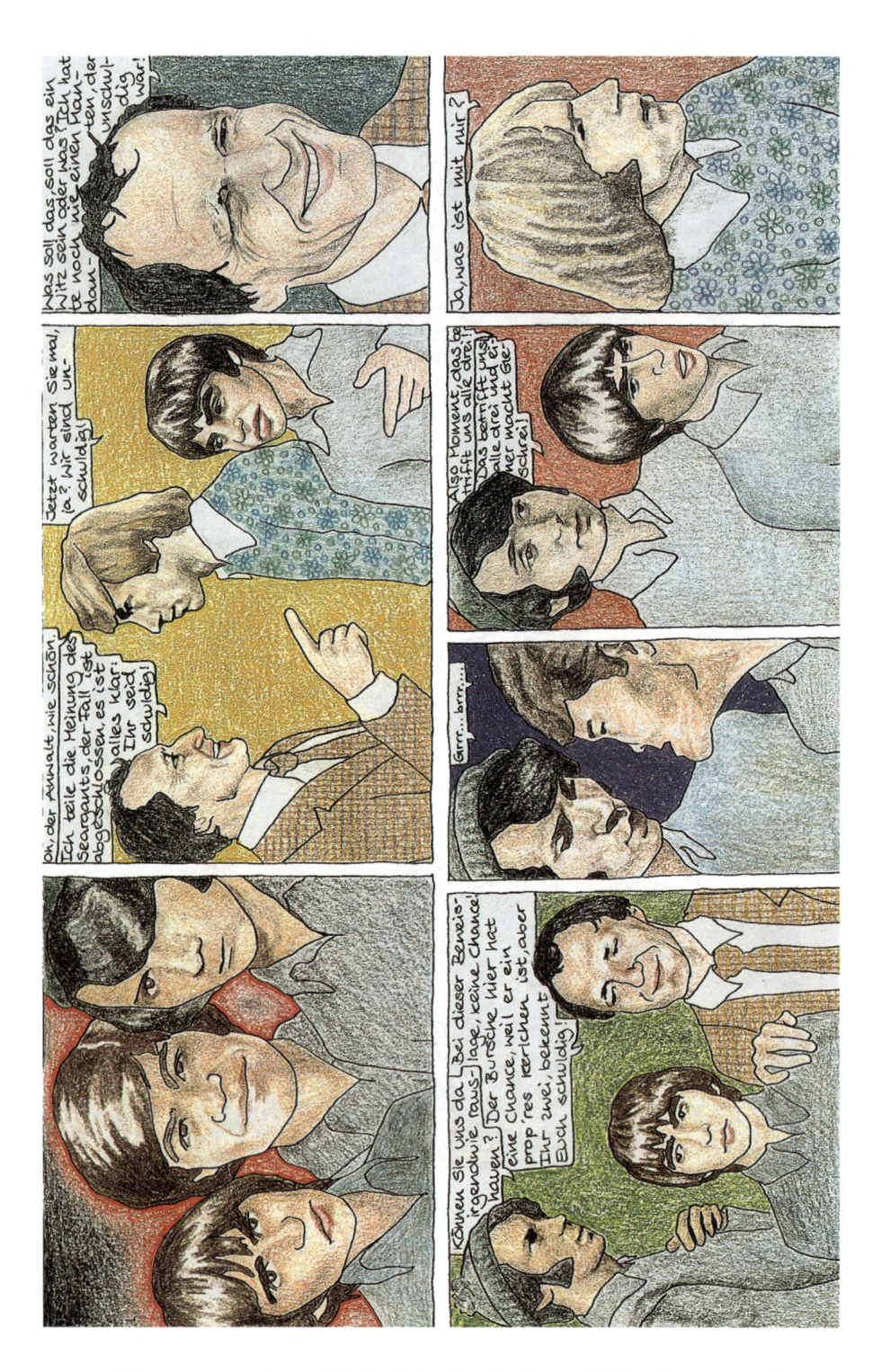

54  Two pages from Valerie's (and sisters) Monkees comic book they did in German.

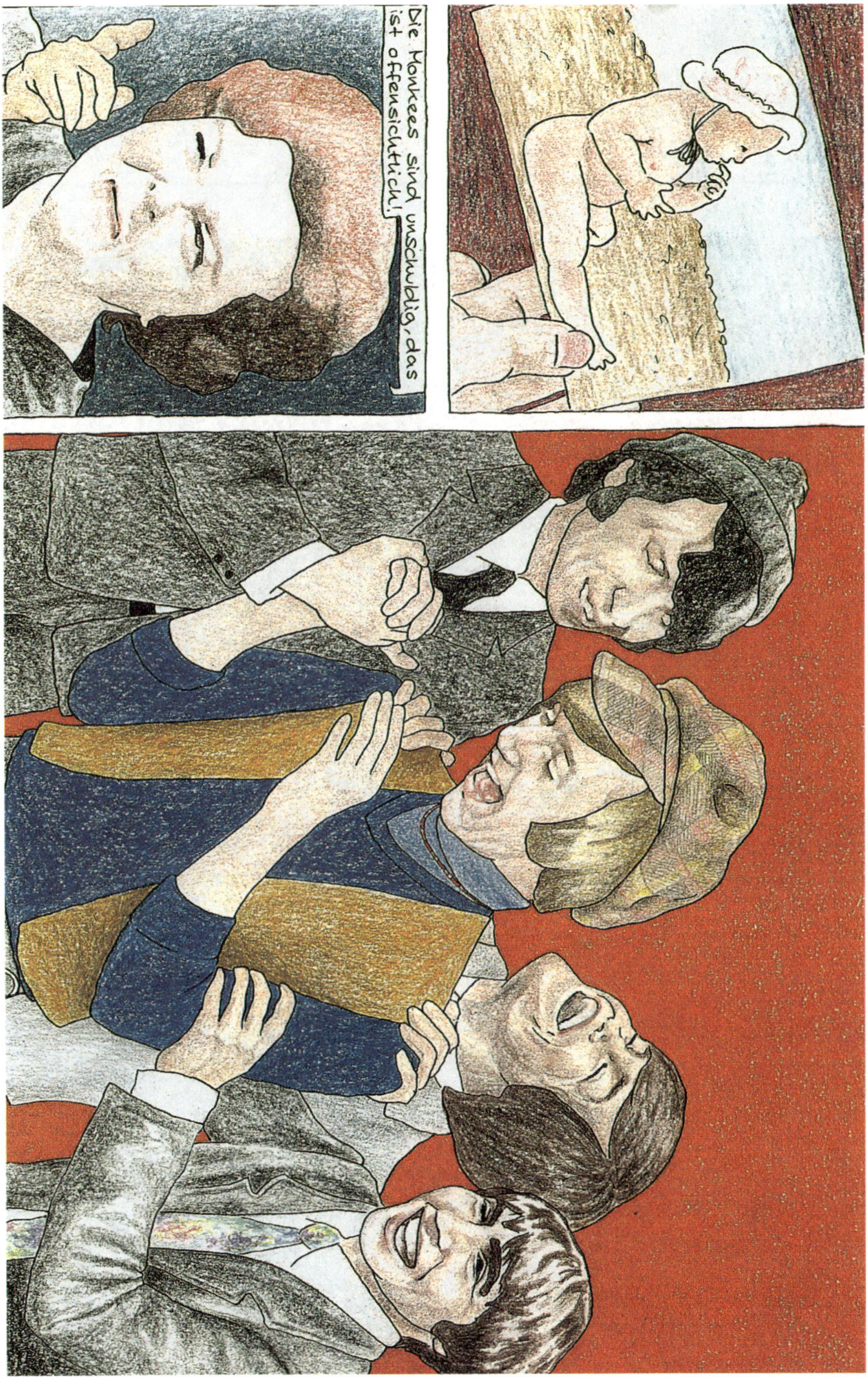
Die Monkees sind unschuldig, das ist offensichtlich!

3 Monkees in action: Peter, Davy & Micky.

lent me his sister's copy of 'Headquarters,' as I didn't own it yet. I found most of their LP's by going to antique stores in the area, and browsing through the record bins. There wasn't any rare record stores around just then.

Over the years I have had the opportunity to get each of the guys to sign things for me. I first saw Peter Tork in 1980. He was touring with a band called 'Cottonmouth' at the time. This was at a show at the Bottom Line in NYC. He signed stuff after the show and he signed my 'Headquarters' cover. Davy Jones is always the fan pleaser....when I met him, he told me to wait until he had some photos taken with some kids in wheelchairs. I finally got a picture with him. Micky signed a CD cover for me, and when I met Mike Nesmith he was playing a C&W club in NYC. I always had great respect and admiration for him and I was very nervous being right there with him."

\*

Abby Alterio runs the Davy Devotees web site. In August of 1999 Davy, himself, gave Abby permission to have the fanclub declared "official." www.geocities.com/davydevotee/dd2.html (this is the address). Also, Abby has a real heart wrenching story later in this book that you will want to be sure to read. In the meantime, here is how Abby came to be a Monkees fan and the President of an official Davy Jones web site.

"My fascination with the Monkees started in 1986/1987 when I was 7 years old. My tastes in music, and everything else, was heavily influenced by my older brother. He was an avid record collector and had the 'Headquarters' album on vinyl. I remember him playing the record and I fell for the music instantly. Around this same time MTV started airing the original TV episodes and I was hooked. We taped each episode and watched them over and over.

So as the years passed, my brother decided it was 'uncool' to like the Monkees and though I remained a Monkees fan at heart , I became a pre-teen and was influenced by the New Kids on the Block. Of course, this didn't last past the age of 15 or so and one day I walked into a Best Buy store and saw the CD box set of the Monkees 'Listen to the Band.' I told my mom I just had to take the money out of the bank so I could buy it. When I played the CD's, so many memories came back to me from being a little kid and spending time with my brother. It was great. I fell in love all over again and have only grown a bigger Monkeemanic through the years. I am now 21 and am married to a man whom shares the same passion for the Monkees as I do. We met in 1996 at an internet gathering of Monkees fans in Merrillville, IN just before a Monkees concert (in the 30th anniversary tour).

I'm a modern day, true Marcia Brady in that I started Davy Devotees when I was 17, never dreaming I'd actually meet Davy or get permission to run his fan-club, though that finally happened because of a lot of belief in what I do and a lot of hard work."

*

The following is a very interesting account of Valerie who lives in Germany, along with her two sisters. They are quite the artists and have created art of the Monkees along with a full-length comic book based on one of the Monkees TV episodes. It was done in the German language, but they are also starting one in English. You can see some of their Monkees art, and some of the comic book here in my book. Here's Valerie's story.

"My sisters and I are German Monkees fans, something that does not exist too much here. When we first discovered them we didn't know anybody else who knew of them, or were interested in getting to know them, so there was 'just us.' We couldn't find anything related to them in the stores, so we stopped a video tape to draw them, the way we were seeing them on TV, just to have pics of them. A few months later we started a big project: a Monkees comic, which we finished after 16 months, not quite half a year ago. We didn't have any English video episodes at first, so we did the comic in German.

Seeing the Monkees in English for the first time was really incredible. I had been so wanting to hear them talk (in their own voices). We were as crazy about them as you can possibly be, while it seemed like we were the only ones in the whole world who knew about them. With a little help from the Internet we found out that this was not the case and even managed to make a few fellow-Monkee-fan-friends in America. Our American friends had different chances to see a Monkee in concert and of course we have always been very, very envious of them. One pen pal wrote me, that she was going to a festival in Tennessee where Davy and Micky were going to be, and somehow I decided that I wanted to go there, too. It was always my biggest wish to see Davy.

To make a really long story short, I really did find myself on a plane not much later, totally unable to believe what I was doing. My online friend had invited me to stay with her for 2 weeks afterwards. When we got to go to Itchycoo I still couldn't believe I was going to see Micky and Davy. I felt very bad about me seeing them without my sisters, but it is still one of my biggest wishes that one day I will get to go to a concert of one of the Monkees together with the two of them.

I kind of went crazy when I saw Micky appear, I was so unbelievably happy. I had the comic book in my hand, but it didn't work out that I could give it to him. All of a sudden Micky was gone and I still had the comic in my hand. I begged the security guards to take it to him, but no matter how much I cried and explained that I had come so far, and what it meant to me, they wouldn't help me. I was so desperate, then this one guy, who looked like George Harrison in the 70's, helped me! He gave me his backstage pass and all of a sudden I was inside and he led me to Micky's little room. I went in there, and there was Micky (sigh) saying, 'Hey! I saw you! You were in the front row, weren't you? Yeah, I saw you....' It seemed very surrealistic, because he was so incredibly kind and friendly to me, so warm and sweet. It was nothing like the way I'd imagine a fan-meets- star meeting. I was deeply impressed by the way he treats little fans like me, I really am. I can't express what this meant to me.

Davy was suppose to be on the next day, but he didn't make it. Oh yeah, I forgot to mention, Micky really seemed to like the comic book, he said he was going to keep it as a treasure….."

*

Tara is the person that Valerie stayed with in the US when she came out from Germany. Who says that birds of a feather don't stick together? Tara is quite the Monkees fan as her story proves. "My friend, Lacey, and I were both underage when we learned that Davy Jones would be performing at a casino an hour away from us in Alton, IL on April 25th, 1998. My aunt agreed to take us in the hopes that we could just get a glimpse of him somehow. When we got there we asked a security guard if Davy was already there and he said yes. So my aunt told us to go in there and see him. My friend and I went in there trying to act like we were suppose to be there. We looked in rooms, went down empty hallways and peeked inside doors but we couldn't find Davy. So we went back outside and told my aunt. She finally agreed that she would come in with us. We only had enough money between us for one ticket and so my aunt stood in line to get a ticket with the idea of getting some photos. Then we ran into a security guard who asked us for ID which we didn't have. We begged him to let us see DavyJones, he said no and laughed. So we sat down on the stairs while my aunt was in line. She began talking to a lady and the lady told her that Davy was downstairs in another room signing autographs. We screamed and we went down there. When we got just outside the room, I saw a camera flash go off and knew he was in there. So I screamed (natural reaction) and everyone stopped talking and looked at us. Davy said "ello" and we got in line to get an autograph. I got so excited that I started crying, which got my friend crying. By the time we got up there we were bawling like babies! But he signed each of our Monkees books and nicely posed for pictures, and even volunteered to take another. How sweet he was!!! I'll never forget that! When I got home, I took off the shirt he touched when he put his arm around me, and hung it up. I haven't worn it since then." Tara has a nice little Davy Jones fan page at: www.geocities.com/Broadway/Balcony/8644 . It is called: Hopelessly Devoted to Davy Jones.

*

The TV show reaches into France, and Aurelie became a fan through it. "I first heard of the Monkees in 1996, but really became interested in them in February of 1999 through the TV show. I liked the good music and the total madness. They changed many things of my way of life. For example, I can't bear today's fashions and music anymore. So blasted (?) are the people who listen to the new wave of music! People now think I am totally crazy. That's true! It's because of the Monkees! I wonder why we do not hear much of them in Europe? (Except in England I guess). Why don't they try to make some concerts here? I'm not really aware about the number of European fans actually.....but I know a few of them."

*

Here is imput from Barbara, from Southern California. "I first became aware of the Monkees in 1965 (1966?). I don't remember exactly if it was through the radio (KHJ), or the TV show, but I know it was at the beginning. I enjoyed the music and always watched the TV show. The Monkees were the first group that I collected albums from. I was just 8 years old at the time and life was basically school and friends. All of my friends liked the Monkees and the usual things like; which of the guys was the cutest, best, etc. Also, collecting Tiger Beat magazine photos. I think about how different it was back then when kids liked a group, and the music compared to today. Also, to buy albums was a BIG deal because it meant a trip to Wallace's Music City (about a half hour away in Torrance) since that was the closest place that sold LPs (not like all the Warehouses, etc. in almost every town now). Now as I'm on the Internet and look at Monkees pages, sometimes I see comments that someone wished they were in Southern California back in the 60's so they'd get to meet stars. I have to think to myself that it wasn't that way...it was no guarantee that you were going to 'run into' stars like the Monkees."

(Editor's note): I have to disagree with Barbara here. It would have to depend on where you lived in Southern California and how much you got out and

Micky & Davy with first wives & children.

where you went. I was living there in the early 70's and I saw and met quite a few stars. In fact once, on a Sunday morning, down on the Sunset Strip, by the old Playboy club in Hollywood, I was walking down the sidewalk with nobody out at all except two people talking together way up ahead. As I got closer one of the people looked just like Davy Jones. And sure enough, it was Davy. I tried to think to myself, as I was approaching them, if I would stop and talk, but I thought I would be too much of an intruder and walked past them. They didn't pay any attention to me as I passed by. I went up ahead a little bit and pretended I was looking in some shop windows, or something, as I watched them talk. I kept trying to decide if I should go up and talk to them, but I didn't feel good about it. The two of them talked for some time and I decided to just go on.

*

Here's some more comments through the Monkee fan network. "For years I knew that the Monkees existed, but I didn't become a fan until 1996, through the TV show. I thought they were fantastic and just so funny from the moment I first saw them, I couldn't think of anything else. I don't know really what was going on in my life then, but the Monkees helped cheer me up."

*

Shane had this to say, "I guess I 'knew' about the Monkees ever since I was a child in the 70's, but really didn't 'discover' them until the wave of MTV nostalgia in 1986. I knew about the songs, the hits anyway, as long as I can remember back. What got me hooked was the television show, when MTV ran the first Monkees marathon. That's when I really became 'aware' of them. The Monkees have affected me in a way no other group/TV show/ pop phenomenon

Micky, Samantha (Mickey's first wife) and Davy.

ever has.  It's like chocolate.  One taste and you're hooked for life.  There had been years before I found the world of fan clubs when I thought I was the only fan left after the wave of popularity in the 80's, but since then I have made so many friends, and seen so many shows (solo and collective), that I am proud to be branded for life!  1986, when I first really discovered the guys, was not a very good year for me.  For starters, I was 13 – the onslaught of adolescence, which is scary to begin with, but worst my parents were going through a rough divorce right about then.  It really affected my sister and I terribly, and the Monkees were a respite from all of that, if only for half hour segments.  I never did see any of the live shows in 86, or 87, but felt a connection with the whole phenomenon all the same.  I never would have believed back then that 10-12 years later, I would have met Micky, Peter and David on numerous occasions and had the chance to talk with Nez online!"

\*

Here is another response from England.  Barbara writes, "My first memory of the Monkees was hearing 'I'm A Believer' on the radio, although I didn't know who it was at first.  It was 1967 and I was nearly 15 years old.  I had one of those small transistor radios which I used to take to bed to hear music from the pirate radio stations.  Then I saw the first episode on the TV a week, or two later and it was WOW! We only had a black and white TV, but I lived for those Saturday evenings.  I cut out a tiny photo of Davy from the newspaper and carried it around for days before sticking it in a diary.  Posters covered my bedroom walls, I bought all the albums, even selling my bike at one stage!  I went to see them in Wembley in London with a friend.  Goodness knows how our parents let us do this at such a young age, especially as we had to find a guesthouse to stay in overnight and also cross London on the tube. But I knew I had to be there. London was full of Monkees fans and we met lots of friendly people. We came home from London in a daze.

During the 1996/1997 touring my husband took me to their concert in Cardiff which was the nearest place for us. I couldn't eat, or sleep for days, and the feeling as we were driving to Cardiff was so amazing, knowing that I was getting nearer and nearer to them. I couldn't believe any of this was happening to me, but it was making me very happy. The concert was all I knew it would be and I didn't want it to end. I bought the programme and saw that there was a fan club address which I joined as soon as I got home. I then obtained pen friends from around the country, as I needed like-minded people to write to, to save my sanity!

So since then its all kept going. I've bought all the music available, and more besides. A group of us went to Lingfield Racecourse and watched David riding and had coffee with him."

*

Stephanie had some interesting things to share. "I first became aware of the Monkees August 30, 1997 while I was babysitting. The Monkees marathon was on TV, either on Nick at Nite, or TV Land. You could pretty much say it was love at first sight. At the time I had an accompanist who would always force me to practice my violin solo (even though she was only a year older than me), and I was given the choice to learn to enjoy music, or go crazy. Well, I chose the former. When I saw the Monkees and heard their music, I REALLY started loving music. Because of that love that they sparked, I've learned 4 new instruments in 2 years – piano, alto sax, oboe and guitar.

Last summer I got the chance to go down to Santa Monica while Peter was playing at Harvelle's with the Shoe Suede Blues. I had flown down there all the way from San Francisco (my cousin and aunt are down there too), and I was so excited to get to see him perform. It was August 23, 1998. But when I got there, it turned out to be a 21 and over club! They wouldn't let me in, but I was allowed to stand outside and I could see him through the window. So, there I was, with my camera, trying to take pictures through the glass. Then a really nice guy came up to me and offered to take a picture inside for me. I was so happy I started crying, either that, or simply because I couldn't go inside. Well, one of the workers there, Katie, saw me, and I heard her trying to convince the other people to let me in. They wouldn't, because I was underage. Katie was then sweet enough to see if she could get Peter to come out on his break to talk to me. And Peter, kind soul that he is, agreed. He autographed his CD for me, and I got a picture with him, but the entire time I couldn't believe what was happening.

Up until the 8th grade I'd always thought I'd go to Stanford University and become a doctor. While I haven't completely rejected that idea, the love of music which the Monkees gave me has made me realize that there are plenty of other things to do with my life. After the impact thry've had on me, I know I'll always cherish the lives of Peter, Davy, Mike and Micky."

*

"My name is Stephanie and I am from Queens, NY. I am a first generation fan and I became aware of the Monkees by watching the first TV episode, and was hooked ever since. I also bought all of their 45's, albums, you name it. Also, TONS of Teen Magazines.

Davy

I use to go into NYC a lot. I live 15 minutes from the city, because back then when any of the rock groups came to NYC the DJ's would say, 'Guess which hotel the groups are in?' So my friends, and myself, and a lot of other fans would wait around the hotels to see our teen idols.

In 1967 I was in the Hilton Hotel lobby on a fall day, just hanging out, and in walked David Jones. He was, and still is, the most beautiful man I have ever met. He came over to my friends and myself and gave us his autograph. He drew a flower and peace sign on mine, along with his autograph. I also saw him running into the Summit Hotel in 1967 with Sally Field. Yes, he ran in and left us with Sally.

Now remember when the Monkees were in NYC and there is a picture of Peter Tork and David Jones sitting on the second floor ledge of the Warwick Hotel and their feet are dangling? Well, I was one of the 500 girls screaming for them to jump. However, only Peter threw down his love beads. The highlight of my life was last December 1998, when I was in Clearwater with some friends and attended the Teen Idol show. We stayed in the same hotel as them. I had the chance, along with two of my friends, to sit down with David at breakfast for 2 hours. He is one of the most interesting men I have ever met. We talked about just everything. I just love the Monkees, especially David. The 13 year old kid in me lights up when I see him."

*

Dona writes, "I am in my 30's and started watching the Monkees when I was 12 years old. I would race home every day to watch them on Channel 44. We did not have a VCR, but my dad knew how much I loved the Monkees so he would tape record the show on a audio, cassette player and I would spend hours listening to the show on my cassette player. I was in heaven! Then, also when I was 12, I decided to start a fan club for the Monkees. It was called Monkee Luvers Ltd. I would ride my bike to the local library and research everything I could about them. Then I used an old typewriter to make my newsletter. I had about 30 members and when checks started coming in for upcoming newsletters, I didn't have any idea what to do! I was only 12 and didn't know what to do with the checks! My newsletter started in 1976 and I was only able to make 3 newsletters, but they were really nice! Now, all these years later, I am still a huge Monkees fan, and always will be. I remember riding my bike to the library, then riding home, typing up a newsletter, cutting out pictures, riding my bike to the copy shop, photocopying as many newsletters as I could afford and then scrounging up enough money to mail them off. It was the best time of my life I think! It seems so long ago! When I finally got a computer, I couldn't believe how much Monkee stuff there was!"

*

Jan, has a nicely done Davy Jones website at: http://www.luvdavy.tripod.com/ and she has some great stories from other fans on it that I've included in the 'Monkees Good Deeds' section of this book. Here is what she shared from her own life, "I first became aware of the Monkees, as best as I can figure out, in 1966 because I discovered the show as soon as it came out. At that time I would have been 10 years old. It seems like I would have had to have been older than that, but apparently not. And I think I just caught the show myself without anyone telling me about it. I quick became obsessed with Davy, and started buying all the albums as soon as they came out. I can still remember the excited feeling I got when I would find out another album was out, and I

71

could rush to the store and buy it. When I use to buy a new album I'd take it to my room and play each song, bit by bit, over and over, and write down the words to it. As soon as it was written down, I would practice singing the song along with the album. I did this with every single song on every single album. I had a battery operated record player, Singer brand, as I recall. I would take it and the albums in the back yard to my swing set, and 'sing and swing' with the girl next door. We did this ALL THE TIME, for hours at a time!! I had pictures of the Monkees on my bedroom wall, like all the other kids, and I dreamed of Davy all the time. I am 43 years old now, and I can still sing every single song from those albums, never missing a word, or even an inflection."

*

One nice thing about Kimberly's discovery of the Monkees is that it gave her and her dad something in common. "I first became aware of the Monkees in 1986 when my parents took me to a concert. And the next morning I saw the show on TV. The Monkees have given me the opportunity to meet new friends, who are now very near and dear to me. They gave my dad and me something in common. And the best thing for me, is they influenced me musically, and also in acting. Peter inspired me to learn to play the guitar, and Davy inspired me to sing. Thanks guys! When I first discovered the guys I was in grade school, and I just wanted to hang out with my friends and have fun. The Monkees made that more fun!"

*

I have met Scott Nickerson and he's a great guy. He has a band and he gave me one of their CDs, and it's good. Scott is a key figure in the Jimmy Buffett Parrothead community, in fact he was instrumental in getting the Parrothead club website network off the ground. It's interesting to see here how Micky Dolenz was such an influence on him. Also, Scott is the first person I have ever met who attended one of the Monkees concerts that Jimi Hendrix opened for.

"I do not recall the year that I first became aware of the Monkees, but it was the year that the first album came out. Frankly, I don't remember whether it was the album, or the TV series that I first became aware of them, but I know I was addicted to the album. I bought every album after that and began playing the drums because of Micky Dolenz. Thirty-something years later I still play drums (etc.) professionally for a living. I'd love to meet him one day and thank him for the inspiration.

I was an 8, or 9 year old kid in grammar school in Asheville, NC when I first became aware of the Monkees. The inspiration to play drums was so strong because of the Monkees that my grandfather put me through 3 years of drum lessons. I played in every school band situation I could get involved in, from marching band to jazz ensemble from grammar school through college. I was one of the lucky ones. I was earning money playing from the time I was 15 (1972) in my own rock band (Medusa, in Griffin, GA) right through to the present day (A1A, The Jimmy Buffett Tribute Show).

A few years ago, I got to meet Peter Tork after his, and James Stanley's show at a small, local club called the Freight Room (R.I.P.) in Atlanta, GA. When I was around 10, or 11 my mom had taken me to see the Monkees live concert at the Charlotte Coliseum in Charlotte, NC, and Jimmy Hendrix opened for them. I told Peter this, and he flipped. He commented, 'You couldn't possibly be that old!' Turns out Hendrix opened for only 3 Monkees concerts that year, which

Alan Green playing for Davy for 'They Made A Monkee Out of Me' book signing.

Davy signing 'They Made a Monkee Out of Me' at: Hickory Hollow Mall, Nashville, TN  3-4-89

Davy signing books, Hickory Hollow Mall  3-4-89

I believe was 1968, before Woodstock put him indelibly into the history books."

*

"My name is Kim (I'm 29) and I have been a fan since about 1987. I saw them first on MTV that summer at a friend's house. I thought they were funny, but what I really liked was the music. The first episode I saw was 'Monsterous Monkee Mash' with the song 'Goin' Down.' This song is still one of my favorites. So, not having MTV myself, I never saw them on MTV again. I was so taken by them, and that they were so cute, Micky being my favorite. I looked into finding out about them, and bought their music. The next year, 1988, they were in syndication. They helped me through some tough times – high school, college, then trying to recover from a eating disorder in the middle of all this. I would always be happy if I watched a TV episode, or listen to their music. I am much better now, healthwise, I think partly because I had something to listen to, or watch that will always be there for me whatever happens."

*

Here's another reply from England. "My name is Michelle, and I'm a huge Monkees fan. I first discovered the Monkees probably around 1974, or 1975 when I was around 4, or 5 years old. I am what is known in the Monkeeworld as a 'Second Generation Fan.' They played the television show on Saturday mornings, and I never missed it. I remember sitting in front of the TV with my bowl of Rice Krispies and watching 'Alias Micky Dolenz' – and wondering where they got that guy who looked just like Micky! (Hey, I was only a kid, gimme a break!). If there was something I didn't want to do, all my mom had to say was, 'Well, the Monkees would do it…..' and it was done! I was instantly in love with Davy – even though I often confused him with Peter (Hey, I was a kid.....they had similar hair...). I thought that it was the best show I ever saw – when I watch them now, I still am amazed at all the 'adult' humor that I didn't catch as a kid, and I wonder how in the world they got away with some of that stuff – very sly. At the time, I thought they were the best thing going – truth be told, I still feel that way. They were funny and crazy and even in the early 70's there still wasn't anything like that show – still isn't actually. It was just so innovative. Obviously, they had a huge impact on my life, in that I run a fan club with my sister-in-law, and we travel whenever we can to see Peter, Davy and Micky (Mike doesn't tour much anymore). We even traveled 300 miles, just to see the Monkeemobile. The TV show doesn't really play as big of a role in my life as it used to (although I still love it, I just don't get to watch it as much as I used to). I am in it for the music now. I have tape after tape of stuff I listen to in my car – generally, the Monkees, or one of them individually, are all I listen to. I love a lot of their solo works, especially Peter (but he is my personal favorite, so that may have something to do with it – all seriousness aside). I really owe my sense of humor to two things in my life, one is my dad and the other is the Monkees. I love the show and I love the music. Always have, and always will."

*

Here's a lengthy account from Claire Powell of Brussels, Belgium, but it has so much interesting information that I wanted to include it in its entirety. "I first became aware of the Monkees in December 1966. It was hearing 'Last Train To Clarksville' on the radio. I loved it! I remember a full front page advert for it on the cover of the influential New Music Express. Until then I'd liked solo artists like Cliff Richard and Cat Stevens. I had never been a Beatles fan. My favorite band had been the instrumentalists backing Cliff, the Shadows.

I was really getting into 'Clarksville' when 'I'm A Believer' was issued. I loved that so much that I went out and bought it. Of course, there was a very orchestrated publicity campaign. The BBC was about to show the Monkees series. I tuned in for the first edition and was hooked. It really was the forerunner of the video. Here were four acheingly, handsome guys. We could watch 25 minutes of them every week and they got a plug for their latest single. I remember the color cover of Davy on a Fab 208. He had very long hair and a suit and collar and tie on. He looked so handsome! He was my favorite.

It was no secret how they were put together. We read about the auditions and thought 'So what?' Ironically in all the Beatles versus Monkees debate, people overlooked the fact that John Lennon is quoted as saying that he loved the TV series. As the hits continued, the Monkees seemed to be flying to the UK to do promotional work when they weren't filming a series. They were hardly ever out of the NME or Fab 208. I think the merchandising wasn't as bad as in the USA. We didn't get the lunch boxes, etc. I was a schoolgirl in the north of England and a bit dreamy about the band. In the end-of-year English exam I chose to write an essay about 'My favorite TV programme' from a set list and guess which one I chose? I got a very good mark as well! I must say that it relied heavily on press releases I'd read and NME articles.

Of course, we girls all had our copies of 'Meet the Monkees' and played them endlessly in between deciding who our favorite Monkee was, and faithfully bought 'Monkees Monthly.' I joined the UK fan club, but after distributing joiner kits it rapidly deteriorated and Keith Mallet came in for a lot of criticism.

# MONKEE NEWS

OFFICIAL PUBLICATION OF THE MONKEES FAN CLUB ॐ DECEMBER 1967

THE MONKEES take a moment from their busy filming schedule to look over the NEW Fan Club Booklet, now available to renewal memberships as well as to new members.

## Hits Million Mark

The new Monkee album, "Pisces, Aquarius, Capricorn & Jones Ltd." has sold over one million copies. The new single "Daydream Believer" and "Goin' Down" has hit over 1½ million.

Only 1968 members eligible to order exclusive Monkee merchandise shown on pages 4 and 5. Be sure to renew your membership when you place your order!

## NEW MONKEE MEMBERSHIP KIT AVAILABLE NOW

The time is now! The ALL NEW Monkees National Fan Club membership kit is now ready and available to all of you who renew your Fan Club memberships.

The new exciting book (each page perforated for easy framing) contains dozens of never-seen-before pictures, in both color and black and white. It is packed full of other surprises that will thrill every Monkee fan.

Of course, NEW members will also receive the kit, but as a current member of the National Fan Club, you are getting this advance announcement.

### Renewal Due

The renewal dues are only $1.50 and here are just a few of the things you will receive in your NEW kit.

. . . Peter has decided to take Japanese lessons with an eye toward the up-coming visit to Japan. All the boys have already recorded promotion spots in Japanese with the help of a Berlitz language teacher.

someone else. They bought Marilyn Schlossberg, their production assistant, a white MGB sports car for her birthday. It was quite a surprise and naturally this birthday turned out to be the most exciting she's ever had.

* Booklet packed full of new never-seen-before pictures.
* Your personal membership identification card.
* Official Monkee Pen
* Membership button
* Monkee school book cover

### New Color Pin Up

The big news is the inclusion of the 4 large color pin ups in this year's NEW kit. The only people that will be able to get these pictures are fan club members.

### So, The Time Is Now!

Fill out the membership form and mail with $1.50 today. Be one of the first in your school to have your NEW kit.

MONKEES FAN CLUB

The Monkees Fan Club's first Newsletter.

The summer of love came and the Monkees went along with it with kaftans and beads, and writing more of their own material. What annoyed me no end, and made me cry was that when UK concerts were announced they were only at Wembley, London. No way would my mother let me go. I was heartbroken. Nowadays, bands would go to arenas all over the country. The music industry didn't seem to like the Monkees, and there was the insidious 'They don't play their own instruments' whisper. Of course, in the beginning they didn't claim to!

My father's work took us to Singapore in June of 1968. I recall one girl asking me on my first day at school which group was my favorite. I told her. She said she liked the Doors. I must admit that I was later to like them, but by now I also liked the Herd and Love Affair, the latter incidentally also suffering from accusations of 'they don't play on their records.' Although we could buy the records, it was hard getting information. NMEs and Fab 208s took 6 weeks to come by sea. No faxes, e-mails or web sites then! In some ways I was fortunate in that the TV series was shown on Singapore TV, but the drip-drip effect came. First of all it was revealed that Davy was married and had a child. (In fact the baby came before the marriage, but we'll gloss over that). Now I would never be Mrs. Jones! How could I cope?! Well, I did. But then came the terrible news. The Monkees didn't exist anymore as a band. I didn't in fact go to pieces. Life went on and I discovered the Moody Blues and thought they were the most marvelous band in the world – which incidentally, I still believe.

I always thought that if the UK fan club had been better organized, perhaps singles after 'Valleri' would have sold better in the UK and the band would have stayed together, but there were deeper problems than that. And suddenly we had no TV series and no

Peter Tork

records to buy. So I got on with my life, finished school and became a computer programmer in the south of England. I then went to work in Brussels, Belgium in May 1978 and have stayed here since. But Monkeeness for me was by no means over. There were occasional bits in newspapers about Micky directing a children's version of 'Bugsy Malone' in the heart of theaterland in London. He and Davy appeared in 'The Point.' Both divorced and remarried. Davy did panto in assorted theaters. We even got to see him on TV in 'Little and Large Show' and on a 'Puzzle Trail' children's quiz. (Far too complicated for me!) And aficionados could check out Mike Nesmith's offerings on vinyl.

I was building up my career and into Barclay James Harvest, Steeleye Span and Neil Diamond when the Monkees had a bit of a resurgence with their 20th anniversary. That went on without Mike for about 3 years. Then it came to the UK in 1989 and I got a ticket for the show at the Corn Exchange, Cambridge. 'Oh, What A Night!' I didn't know what to expect, certainly not the sleek, professional show from the trio, but why should I have thought that we'd get anything less than 100% from them? I loved it. I had sneaked a camera in and during the final song I snapped away. I didn't get any stagedoor meeting, or anything, but I was happy! In the tour programme was an ad for the UK fan club. It was not run by a Keith, but a Kirk (White). I joined, I must say, as one of a select few, but we grew and the club's quarterly newsletter, of which there had been four issues before I joined, just got better and better as membership grew.

Kirk always divided news into two distinct areas, what each (ex)Monkee was doing as a solo project, and what might be happening as a reunion of the trio. I was amazed at what merchandise was available from assorted sources, and always seemed to be sending off cheques to the UK, or States. Books came out like 'Mutant Monkees,' and I remember how thrilled I was when I got my copy autographed by Davy. It said, 'Claire, the moment I saw you I swear...' So, he was acquainted with the Gilbert O' Sullivan hit. Kirk is a resourceful fellow. He was then living in Devon and had a dream of bringing Davy over for a club-only cabaret. It took about 6 months of planning, the price had to be increased (to a modest 15 pounds) and the venue changed (for the better I think) from a social club to a posh hotel in Torbay. I bought a ticket and could not believe that I'd be a part of an intimate evening which would be on October 14th, 1993. But the day came and I flew over from Brussels and got the coach to Torbay, and arrived at the hotel in this charming Riviera-like town. Davy's two fellow musicos were setting up the instruments. I met Kirk, and devout fan Lyn Jeffs from Wales, amongst others which was a great pleasure. Marcus had set up a stall of memorabilia and I duly handed over the dosh for assorted items.

I relaxed in my room and got ready for the show. No place was far away from the stage in that ballroom. When 7:30 pm came Kirk got up and announced that the evening was cancelled as Davy didn't feel like doing the show. Oh, what a sense of humor he had! Davy came in wearing blue slacks and a black shirt. He looked fit and healthy. I have written the set list of what he sang that night, but the gaps in between songs became longer as he reminisced and told jokes. I could not get over how good he was, and how near I was to him! There was an interval and we could wait for an autograph, and photograph opportunity with him. He was so good-natured about it. Being 4 ft. 10 ins. Tall, I looked correct next to him! Part two started and that was terrific. He acknowledged fans from as far away as Holland and Japan. What could he end on but 'Daydream Believer'? And yet the night was not finished. The bar was still open and as we ordered drinks he came and mingled amongst us. It was extraordinary. Nobody broke any unwritten rules of etiquette and it was superb. Davy left (with Jim and Jerry to find a curry, we were later told). I met them in the lift and treated them like normal people. How I ever got to sleep that night I don't know. I'd met one of my heroes! I was up early to catch the coach, then plane home. I kept reliving the previous night. Many of us took time to send 'Thank you' cards to Kirk in gratitude for all his hard work. We later found out how much effort it had been, not the least was on the technical side looking for the right sort of leads for the mikes that Davy required. And that was that. Then near Christmas, I received an envelope from America. I knew that I knew the handwriting, but couldn't place it. I opened it up and what should be inside but a signed photo from Davy, plus a short letter telling me about his stint in a show in Atlantic City, New Jersey. I was ecstatic!

I treasure my photos from that 1993 evening, and also the penfriendships with Lyn and Frances Chaffrey. How could we know where we'd go from there? Well, we didn't know that we'd met up in 1996. It started with a call to me in early March from Kirk. He had been told that the Monkees would be at the Sportspaleis in Antwerp (up the road from where I live) on April 26th and he was having trouble getting tickets. Could I help? Of course I could, but I was suspicious; Sortspaleis? A 17,000 seater. I suspected that it was a golden oldies night with about 10 acts each allowed 20 minutes. I had a number to ring and would phone the next day during office hours. I was not wrong. But 20 minutes was 20 minutes more than we got in 1995, so I got the tickets as requested, and put in supplementary orders as they came in. Unfortunately, tickets had already gone on sale so we

Micky Dolenz in action.

were on the 37th row. It was indeed a golden oldies show and the Monkees would be the duo of Davy and Micky, backed by Jerry and others.

It was great to meet up with all these people again, and having a chat with Micky Dolenz before the show was unreal. He wasn't thrilled with arrangements. He had every right to be. The Troggs weren't bad, but Slade II were awful. The Monkees, as such, would be the penultimate act, making way for Procul Harum. We were very lucky, the guards let us stand at the front of the Stage for the Monkees. It may have been a short and sweet set, but we loved it.

What next? Well, it was the 30th anniversary of the Monkees and it had been hoped that there would be a few reunion concerts, if not a USA tour. That didn't materialize, but the lovely Kirk, and his lady Sue got on the phone to me. The four Monkees were reuniting for a UK tour in March of 1997. The fan club was allowed first pickings at the tickets before a certain date. Which did I want to go to? I had in fact already got tickets for a Moody Blues tour in the UK for much of the same dates, so it was pretty obvious that I would only go to the Birmingham, Cardiff and Wembley ones. Sue could tell tales about the on-off saga of the Belfast date. A second Wembley one was added to end the tour, but sadly I had already paid my non-refundable, non-transferable Apex fare on the Eurostar, so I couldn't stay for that, but three concerts would be terrific! I knew all this by Christmas so I could go into 1997 excited. To be honest, the sheer logistics of taking in one performance of 'Heathcliff' with (by now) Sir Cliff Richard, one Steeleye Span concert, several Moody Blues gigs and the Monkees took up some time. Lyn was a great help organizing hotels.

So that was how I came to be in Cardiff on March 12th. I met up with Lyn, Frances and her husband Dave, and other fans who chatted about their Monkee experiences. Imagine our surprise when we realized that we were in the same hotel as the Monkees! Peter Tork was playing something jazzy on the hotel piano, and was that not Mike Nesmith having afternoon tea over there and reading some weighty tome?! But, being polite, we didn't bother them. Somehow we got after-show passes....I didn't delve too deeply into the how. Incredible! Then a call came through. A lady journalist wanted to see us and talk about our love of the Monkees.

Showtime came. We were on the front row. To be honest I could have done without the warm-up act Nancy Boy, which included Mike's son and Donovan's. I was there for the Monkees and it was incredible. The audience was split about 50/50 male/female and had all ages. As 'I'm A Believer' started, young men rushed to the front and started doing an incredible backwards dance. We all got on our feet and surged forward, and never sat down again. And there was Mike! It was good to see him on stage, to say the least. I really appreciated the solo turns each Monkee did. If I had any criticism of the show it would be only the sins of omission. No 'I Wanna Be Free.' But, hey, it had been marvelous.

Our passes got us backstage. Pap Nez had a cold and didn't join us, but the trio did and signed autographs and we joked with them. A photographer appeared, but I thought no more of that. I hadn't dared sneak a camera in in case there was a strict banning policy. 'Oh, What A Night!' as Davy had sung. Micky was at the hotel bar with the Moodies road manager – he was there 24 hours before they would be. I stayed for the MBs while the gang carried on to other venues. I rejoined them at Birmingham. I was informed that a photo of Davy, with his arm around me, had appeared in 'Wales On Sunday' so I was anxious to see it, but I was captioned as Frances! It was, in fact, her and Dave's wedding anniversary, and what better way to spend it than a splendid Monkees gig, a sold-out one at the enormous NEC? Next morning we were a bit annoyed to pick up a 'Birmingham Post' and read a negative and factually inaccurate review of the gig.

So to Wembley, the indoors arena, not the outside stadium where the 1967 concerts had been. What can I say? Full again. In a show of highlights, I think I would have to single out Mick's tour de force on 'Goin' Down.' There was a camera to relay the show onto video screens for those at the back. During the inevitable finale, 'Daydream Believer,' the camera was turned on us in the audience as we all joined hands, held them aloft and waved them in time. It was a very emotional moment. And that was it for me. I will admit to envying my friends who would have one more concert.

Sadly, Mike did not feel able to do some USA shows and the quartet has not been seen together since, but we can hope. A year 2000 reunion? A 35th anniversary reunion? The Monkees might not have been brought together as existing friends, but they were an incredible phenomenon in the late 60s, they either were given, or wrote some classy songs, and why do I have a sneaking suspicion that we haven't heard the last of them yet?"

*

MJ wrote, "I first became aware of the Monkees in 1986 via MTV. They had the first of a few Monkee marathons in February 1986. My impressions of the Monkees were that they were talented and funny, and I really enjoyed the TV show. My 'favorite' Monkees oscillated between Micky (I loved his curly

Davy on stage.

hair) and Peter (he seemed more like a real hippie). They also had a tremendous effect on me and my life. I got my drivers license because I needed to know how to drive to get to shows. As a result of going to Monkees shows I got to see LA, Lake Tahoe and Philadelphia, just to name a few places. I live in the Midwest and had not traveled much prior to becoming a Monkees fanatic in the 1980s."

*

Mike had this to share, "In September of 1978, when I was young, I saw my first Monkees episode (Dance Monkees Dance). I was raised in a household where shows such as this weren't viewed, so this was really my first experience with a show about 'long-haired weirdos' in a rock and roll band. Being musically inclined, I found myself enthralled with the show and began to watch it religiously. Being 1978, and being a child, I did not have the resources to find Monkees music and was thrilled to discover that my close friend had 'More Of…' and 'Headquarters.' This fueled the fire! Unfortunately, my family relocated to Michigan in December of 1978 and stations in our new hometown did not air the Monkees. But, summer reruns came along! My Monkeemanicness was in full swing that summer as I was given, as a birthday gift, Arista's 'The Monkees Greatest Hits' LP. Once fall came around, the Monkees were yanked from the TV show lineup, not to return until the late 80s. All was quiet on the Monkees front until early 1986. I always considered myself a fan up to that point, but once all of the original albums were again available, as well as the trio being in the spotlight, I really went full swing. Being a Monkees fan inspired me to learn to play the guitar around this time, and I have been an amateur musician since. The Monkees also inspired me to look more at the music of the 60's (as opposed to the pop drivel I was listening to at the time), and beyond. So, in other words, I attribute much of who I am...a music lover, a musician...to the Monkees. The Monkees are also a major stress reliever for me. When I'm feeling stressed out, whether from work related or other issues, I can usually pop in a Monkees CD or video, and just be happy and relax."

\*

Gail from Rockville, Maryland had a lot of informative things to share, "My younger childhood days were days of confusion. In 1964 my mother passed away (I was 8 years old), I was separated from my biological brothers and sister and became a part of a family that just wasn't mine. I don't have many fond memories around the years following 1964, But I do remember the Monkees. I saw life as they saw it, or should I say I started to: 'Fun, innocent, and it was ok to be silly.' Of course, everyone had a favorite, and mine was David. He became my hero. The guy that made it even though he was separated from his family at a young age. As a hero - he lived in California (another planet it seemed) and I lived in Maryland. He was an unreachable hero, surely one that I would never have the chance to meet...so I thought.

In 1988 I heard he was autographing at a nearby mall his then, new book 'They Made A Monkee Out of Me.' I just happened to have a copy so I went to the mall. I waited in line with a couple of hundred of people and got his autograph. A short encounter, but I was walking on clouds.

In 1996, I saw the Monkees perform, and a buried passion came alive. After the show I happened to see the bus that David was on go into a hotel parking lot. I pulled in also, and my friend and I stood outside the bus waiting for them to exit. Micky came off the bus first and went straight to the hotel. David came off next and was headed to the hotel until another fan asked him for his autograph. David stopped and signed his book then I handed him an old 'David Jones' Colpex album and exclaimed, 'I have been a fan of yours for a very long time, could I please have your autograph?!' David took the album and autographed it. When I looked at him I saw how tired he was - actually, exhausted would be a better word. At that point I think my childhood infatuation towards him turned to admiration. For though, he was exhausted he took a moment to give me an autograph. Nobody 'important' was close by and he could have blown us off. My respect for him grew even deeper.

After the concert I went home and went through the tour program. I wrote to anybody that could tell me more about the Monkees and David. I learned about the fan clubs and the concerts that had been going on, and the one's that would be. I thought for 30 years that the guys were nowhere to be found except for re-runs, boy! was I wrong! I even bought a computer so I could go online!

So I got the 'fever,' as well as the touring list. I followed David with the Monkees a whole summer whenever I could. I went to his solo concerts, and then followed him the summer of the Teen Idols concerts. I still search his web page for upcoming concerts and will keep going as long as he performs. He's always been kind to me and has always given me a few minutes of his time. I've never been able to tell him about the impact he's made on my life."

(Editor's note): Gail wrote the following which appeared in Abby's publication 'Davy Devotees' in the August 1998 issue, "I had met Davy once before at hissolo concert in Northumberland, PA. We spoke for a minute or two backstage before I went back to my motel. But, it was nothing like I would experience a

Mike & Micky at the Hollywood Walk of Fame ceremony.

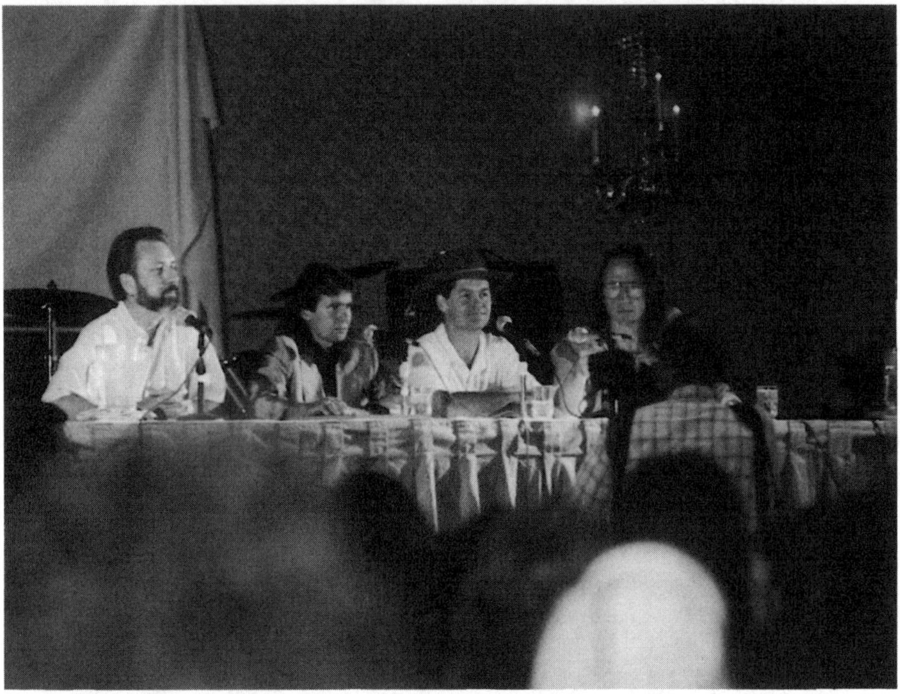

The Monkees at the Hollywood Walk of Fame
Press Conference.

few months later.

I did 'by chance' meet him at the hotel we were staying in at Myrtle Beach. While he was passing by my car we exchanged a few words. At one point I was reading a hotel guide to decide if I should stay at a hotel on the way home instead of driving all the way through. After he had finished packing, he walked over to my car to see what I was reading. When I told him 'just a hotel guide,' he seemed quite concerned and asked me if I was going home that night. It was already 11:30 pm and it was a 9 hour drive back to Maryland. I told him no, and that it was for the following day. He then offered me his room saying, 'We're leaving at 1:00 am if you need a room. You can have mine.'

I don't know if I was in shock, or just comatose from driving all day and then attending the concert but I told him, 'Oh no, that's okay. I already have a room here.' Once I convinced him that I was not driving home, I pulled out one of my scrapbooks, warned himI saved everything, and showed him a few things I had. Afterwards, he went about his way and I left momentarily to 'gas up' my car for the trip back to Maryland.

When I returned, David was standing by the hotel door signing autographs for another fan. When I got my car parked he walked over to it and exclaimed, 'I was going to give you a 'special' autograph and picture of me, but I thought you had left so I gave it to another girl.' After a brief pause he added, 'I think I have another one on the bus. Let me check on my daughter and walk over with me.

So, I waited and when he returned from inside the hotel we walked over to the bus. He reached in a bag and pulled out an 8 x 10 black and white picture of himself. He was stating how good it was while I was awestruck that he was giving it to me! He called it a proof and said he wasn't sure if he was suppose to give it away or not but then said, 'Oh, well.' He asked me for my name again and how I spelled it. After handing me the picture we talked with another fan before he stated he was tired and was going to go 'bunk' on the bus. We went our separate ways and retired for the night. Actually, it was already morning.

As David would say, 'Unbelievable!' I sometimes think that until I open my scrapbook to remind myself that it really happened. I think everyone throughout their life dreams about meeting their idol and I know I have. After attending 11 concerts, including some Monkees shows, taking hundreds of pictures and accumulating enough stuff for 2 scrapbooks, I finally met my idol in an informal manner. I realize how fortunate I have been for I've only caught onto the concerts and fan clubs as of 2 years ago. People have told me that they would have 'died' to have been in my position. But, you know, I feel like I finally got to meet a long awaited friend rather than an idolized entertainer. I found Davy to be very personable, considerate, and down to earth. I'll treasure that picture forever. I couldn't believe he offered the picture and I never asked!"

*

Here is another touching account of how the Monkees helped a fan, Shawna, through a rough period in her life. "I first became aware of the Monkees around 1987, or 1988. I was so small that I'm not exactly sure what year it was. My mother watched the show when I was very small. She had all the LP's and we used to listen to them together. When they were on Nick at Night a few years ago, I became a full-fledged Monkeefanatic. When I was smaller, Micky impressed me the most. But now Mike is my favorite.

Peter seemed 'dumb' as he was portrayed on the show until I saw him in concert in 1997. I had never seen any of them outside of the television context, and that made a real impression on me. Micky seemed rather arrogant (nothing against him, I love him to death), and Peter seemed like a real person. I've never seen Mike in person, but his personality in his writing and on the show always made him appear very intelligent, caring and confident. The Monkees have had a tremendous affect on me. They have changed my life. From their shows I have learned to get away from the troubles of the real world and go have fun. Their carefree music and comedy is just what I need sometimes. Well, I won't go into all the details of what was going on in my life when I first learned of the Monkees. That would take me hours. My parents were having troubles, life was really up in the air. My father was incarcerated for awhile.....Turbulence. Then I discovered them. They've helped me cope. I was unsure of where we'd be living, I was unsure if I was going to be able to stay with my mother....It was a rough time. The Monkees are truly a gift. I love them all very, very much. I truly love them. They have changed me. God sent them and their music to me just when He knew I needed something."

*

Janet in Pittsburgh had this to share, "I am a fan who goes back to the beginning. I became a fan through the TV show, I was only 12 years old. Although I adored all the guys, the first time I saw Micky Dolenz I was hooked on the show. I loved his great sense of humor, and his singing voice. I can't tell you just how much I enjoyed and loved him. My brother use to argue to shut the show off, but I protested. We only had a black and white TV at the time. My father was no where to be found, it was just my mother and brother at the time. I was a shy girl, and did not have many friends, so the Monkees were a bright spot in my life at the time. I looked forward to the show every Monday night. They made me feel so happy. I liked the Beatles, but their music was a blurr, and I didn't even appreciate music till the Monkees, and didn't know how much I loved music until them. My brother bought 'I'm A Believer,' the 45 record at the time, even though he said he didn't like them. He is a year older than me. I ran out and bought 'Pleasent Valley Sunday' and 'Valleri.' I even came across a paper record I didn't even know was still around the house. I always tried to draw the Monkees logo shaped like a guitar on all my notebooks, and things for school. I never could get it right. One day in grade school, someone wrote the name on the board, Monkees, for our singing teacher who was a nun. She said that is not how you spell monkey, and everyone said that's how they spell it. We had to explain that they were a singing group. I don't think she knew who we were talking about at all. I had Micky's and Davy's picture on the bedroom wall for many years. I still have them in a scrapbook from 1967. I bought a magazine called 'Here We Are' for only a dollar which I still have, and a '16' magazine, also from 1967. I didn't even know they were singing at concerts, in my hometown and all around the country. I was too young, I guess, to understand. All I know is the joy I received from that show, and the music. It was so wonderful for me as a young girl coming of age and starting to grow up, and discovering something about my personality at the time. It's so nice to have known them through their music, and the TV show. I always remember them by it. They gave me laughter and excitement and joy, and I'll never forget them and the memories they gave me back then. When you're 12-13 years old you really see things in a different light, it was like magic, and the memories will always be there to look back on."

\*

Here's material from Debbie in Thurso, Scotland, "I first heard about the Monkees in 1997. I had seen an advert about the new Monkees Greatest Hits CD and I begged my mother to let me buy it. I also heard that the Monkees were going to be on Channel 4 here, but at that time I didn't know anything about them. The first episode I saw was 'Royal Flush.' I was convinced that Davy Jones was American because to me, he sounded like someone from New York or California. I liked everything about them. Their look, their slang, the music. They were so different from the other bands I'd heard. This was music you could sing along with and click your fingers to. I was still at school and in two professional productions at the time, so I didn't have time to watch them properly. But when I did, the more episodes I watched the more I fell in love with them. It's because of the Monkees that I have made several American friends whom I keep in touch via email, and four wonderful English penpals. And although I thought he was American, Davy Jones is still my favorite of all the Monkees."

\*

Lynne in England had this to share, "I first became aware of the Monkees at the end of 1966 when I was looking through the television programme magazine to see what was on. I saw this horrible black and white photo of these four rough looking guys and decided that I did not want to see the show. My brother and I argued about whether or not we would see this new programme, and as usual mum gave him his own way and we saw the show. My brother hated it, but I was well and truly hooked within the first few minutes. Although I like all four of the guys, I felt a certain something extra for Micky Dolenz. He has a wonderful sense of humor, sparkling eyes and a brilliant smile. I was delighted to discover a few weeks

Davy with unidentified fan

later that I had already fallen for Micky years before when he played Corky in Circus Boy.

My three friends Valerie, Pauline and Angela had also seen the show and fallen for the guys. So the Monkees became the focus point of our friendships. I came from a large family where there was not much money to spare, but most of what I had went on Monkee merchandise. I bought all the Monkees Monthlies, girl magazines, bubblegum cards and all the singles. I had two annuals and the first two LP's for Christmas. I joined the fan club and found a penpal through one of the girlie magazines. Donna lived in Les Mesa in California. We wrote to each other for about 16 years.

At the time I was 13 and a half. A lot of my time was spent focused on the Monkees. I would sit in my room with my dog and listen to their music over and over. I watched every single episode. I sometimes felt like I lived from one Saturday to the next just to see the Monkees on TV. Even being glued to the TV just in case an advertisement came on, and watching all the news reports whenever one of them came to England, just to get a glimpse of them. They were more visual than any other group at the time because of the TV show, so I felt like I had come to know them in a more personal way. At the time I did not understand, or really care about how the group got together. I did not want to believe any of the criticisms that were leveled at the Monkees, and tore up anything that I read that I did not like. I would defend the Monkees at every opportunity I got. Often having arguments with my brother's friend who was into the Beatles and the Stones. I often argued with my mum too for having my music too loud, or spending my money on Monkee stuff when I should have been buying clothes. I was not allowed to see them in 1967, but really envied those who did, which included my friend Barbara.

Peter and Davy (on far right)

I can remember being really upset when Peter left, but was also very pleased that it was not Micky. I stayed an avid fan right up until the end when they sort of just faded out of my life. I think they faded away quicker in England because we did not have continuous access to them in the way that American fans did. During the early 1970's the only Monkee I heard about was Mike with his new band, but I was never really a fan of his so I was not interested in his new band either. Life goes on and I married and had a child. It was through watching TV with Aaron that I discovered that Micky was living in England directing. I loved watching Metal Micky with Aaron, I can remember on more than one occasion wishing that Micky was in the show so that I could see him. During this time I did not know what any of the other guys were doing.

In 1989 I was at my parents house flicking through the local newspaper when I saw an advertisement for a Monkee concert. I did not read the advertisement properly and just thought that this was just one of those tribute bands which were around at the time. You can imagine my surprise and shock when I read the advertisement again the following week and it finally sunk in that it was the REAL Micky, David and Peter that were going to perform at the Colston Hall in Bristol on April 1st, 1989. I could not get down there fast enough to buy two tickets. I walked on air for weeks, hardly believing that I was going to see the Monkees in concert at long last, a dream come true. I could not get anyone to come with me, so I took my son Aaron who was then 13. He was into rap and was pleased when the guys did a rap number at the end of the show. I loved every minute of it. Money was still pretty tight so I only bought a programme at the concert. I joined the fan club and started writing to a very nice lady who lived in Lancashire in California. After

Valerie & her two sisters, Corinna & Marlene, who did the German Monkees comic book.

the Monkees split she followed both Micky and Peter around California attending the various venues they were working at. Patti sent me photos of Micky and Peter and all the up to date information. During this period I now had two children, I was doing voluntary work for a childrens charity called Barnardos and I was taking a computer course.

In 1997 my husband arrived home and announced that the Monkees were touring England again. I dashed around like a headless chicken for days trying to buy a ticket to see them. Once again I had problems finding anyone to come with me so Aaron, now 21, came again. We saw the concert at the Cardiff Int'l Arena on March 12th. It was breath-taking, even Aaron was impressed. He said that he couldn't believe that four old men could put on such a long and lively performance. I went on to join the fan club again, regretting having let them slip away again. I found another penpal whom I have developed a good relationship with.

I am quite a shy person so I find meeting new people difficult. I also have never traveled alone before, but in October 1997 I found myself traveling to London to met Barbara, whom I had only been writing to for a few months. We spent the weekend staying in a guest house in London, had a fantastic time at the Monkee convention watching videos, listening to music, buying Monkee stuff and meeting other passionate Monkee fans. I see us having a passion, not an obsession. I have since visited Barbara in Cornwall four times, and she is about to visit me for the fourth time. We have been to three Monkee conventions in England and are hoping to go to the one in LA in September 2000. I have also made other friends that I write to, Helen in Ireland, Maria in Scotland, Kristy in Frome, Suzie and Scott in the States. I met all these people at the convention, except Suzie whom I have yet to meet. By the way, I kept all my Monkees merchandise that I had collected in the 60's. I could not part with this important part of my teenage years. I am not sure how the Monkees affected me back in the 60's, but 30 years on, I know they helped open up my life. I have done things, visited new places and met some wonderful people through the Monkees."

\*

Monkee fan, Heidi had some touching things to share on how the group helped her during a very hard time, "I first became aware of the Monkees around 1986 through my older brother. He was a fan when they were being shown on MTV. He use to watch the reruns in the 70's as well. I watched the Monkees on MTV with my brother whenever he would baby-sit me. I don't remember a whole lot about the episodes, but when I watch them now, certain memories come back of that time. My brother also had a few Monkees albums on tape that I would listen to whenever I had a chance. Whenever he was gone to work, or school I would sneak into his room and take his Walkman and Monkees tapes (I remember him having 'Headquarters' and 'Then and Now: The Best of The Monkees'). I was only about five years old and I would sing and dance all over the house to Monkee tunes. Needless to say, my mother and other adults thought it was strange that a five year old enjoyed jamming to the Monkees every waking moment. My brother was often puzzled as to why his batteries were so low in his Walkman when he would come home! During this time in my life, my mother and father were arguing quite a bit. Eventually, my mom left my dad and moved out with me and my brother. We left nearly everything behind and moved down south. It was a very confusing time for me. One of the things that stands out the most during that time, that helped me the most, was listening to the radio. Even though

I was very young, I had a desire to try and escape the chaos that was going on around me. My brother's radio was my constant companion. I remember being in our little house in Tennessee, where we hardly had anything, and listening to the Monkees on my brother's Walkman until the batteries were so low Micky began to sound like a bass! I remember being so happy listening to their music. At six years of age I would go dancing around on the front porch singing 'Pleasant Valley Sunday." I laugh today when I think about the lyrics I used to sing for the songs on 'Then and Now.' I never could figure out the part in 'Pleasant Valley Sunday' where Micky sang 'status symbol land.' When it got to that part I would just sing 'Daddadada...LAND!' I was pretty depressed as a little kid and I think listening to the Monkees made me happier. When I was young, I wanted so badly to be a singer, or an actress. I'd be in my room and pretend that there was an audience in front of me while I sange Monkees songs. The Monkees brought happiness into my life during a time when everything seemed lost to me. Their music provided an escape for me. Helping me to use my imagination, and discover a talent. My junior high, voice teacher said that my great musical tonal memory was due to listening to music at a young age. I love singing to Monkee tunes to this day. My life has gotten a lot better since that time in the middle to late 80's. I will forever be eternally grateful to the Monkees for helping me through a difficult period of my life. Thanks to them for helping a little girl to dream."

## The Monkees in Concert
### Sat. January 21, 1967  8:00 p.m.

January 21, 1967 was the day I got to see the Monkees live in concert. It was also special because the TV program decided to film it for an actual Monkees episode entitled 'Monkees on Tour.' It was broadcast as the last episode of the first season. When I was watching the TV show I said to my mom that it looked an awful lot like the concert I had seen there in my hometown of Phoenix, Arizona. Then when they showed the Monkees at the place they were staying in Phoenix, Mountain Shadows Resort, I knew beyond a shadow of a doubt that it was all shot there, in my home town! That made it all the more exciting.

While doing this book I had another nice surprise. I met someone else who had been to the very same concert as I. Karen S. from Scottsdale, Arizona was there and she went one up on me......she got over to Mountain Shadows Resort and stalked the guys, or to be more exact, she stalked Davy. First, here is Karen's account of her time just before the Saturday night concert.

"At 14, my first sight that Monday evening in 1966, of

Davy Jones, and he immediately stole my heart. Had to have been the British connection. Back then, anything British was cool, and it is known that was all part of the reasoning of the powers that be at NBC to put him in the show (not taking away from his talent as an actor, that much was obvious even to my little teenage brain). I loved the show from the first minute, and I was glued, inches away from the television screen, every Monday night. Nothing could take me away from that set! That half hour always seemed to fly by in nano seconds! I think it was the only time in my life I ever looked forward to a Monday!

It never occurred to me at that stage that they weren't a real band, but I never dreamed they would go on tour, much less to a desert town like Phoenix, Arizona. After all, the Beatles never came here! So when a concert tour was announced, and Phoenix was included, I was in heaven! I waited impatiently for tickets to go on sale, and I remember having to order them by mail. It was an interminable period of time to get those tickets and I was ecstatic to see I had 10th row! (Not realizing 10th row for something like this would still put us a great deal away from the stage, with all the security involved). I probably should mention that I was going to this concert with my best Monkee pal, Marilyn, who I met that first year in high school. Marilyn was a Peter Tork fan, so there was no competition there! As the concert drew nearer, I was getting pretty excited. There are no words to describe the feeling to seeing my favorites in person.

On January 20, 1967, I was listening to the radio (KRUX-AM) the night before the show. The Monkees had all gone down to the radio station and were playing records, and generally creating havoc. I was stunned when they announced they were staying at the Mountain Shadows Resort in Paradise Valley, a small ritzy suburb of Scottsdale. They actually INVIT-

ED everyone to come down! As soon as I heard this, I flew out of my bedroom and begged my parents to take me down there. Of course they said no. I screamed, ranted and raved and had the biggestt tantrum of my life. All the tears and carrying on would not change their minds! I was devastated. I do not know how I ever fell asleep that night, but I know I cried myself to sleep. But I should have known. I've got the greatest father in the world! First thing Saturday morning, he knocked on my bedroom door and asked me if I wanted to go to Mountain Shadows for breakfast! I dressed in my best dress for school and was ready to go in minutes!

When we arrived at the hotel, I didn't see too many people around. We went into the restaurant and were seated. The waitress came and took our order (did I eat? I don't remember). My dad then asked her about the Monkees and she told him they had just left the table that was next to the one we were sitting at! Oh my heart! It was broken for the first time! After the meal, my dad and I just walked around the resort, trying to figure out where they could be. (I felt pretty secure with an 'adult' with me. No one bothered us). We finally saw a group of people near one of the pool areas, and could see off in the distance that we were close. Mike was standing at his arcadia door inside his room and motioned with his cigarette, to offer it to my dad. He turned him down! I couldn't believe it! He didn't have to SMOKE IT! There was no going back to get that cigarette.

Since we saw so many security guards around, I thought my chances of getting near them were not that good. We walked around to the parking lot area and I saw a group of people standing near a section of rooms. My dad let me go off alone, and he just went to the car and smoked and waited. He didn't give me any kind of time limit (didn't I say he was the coolest

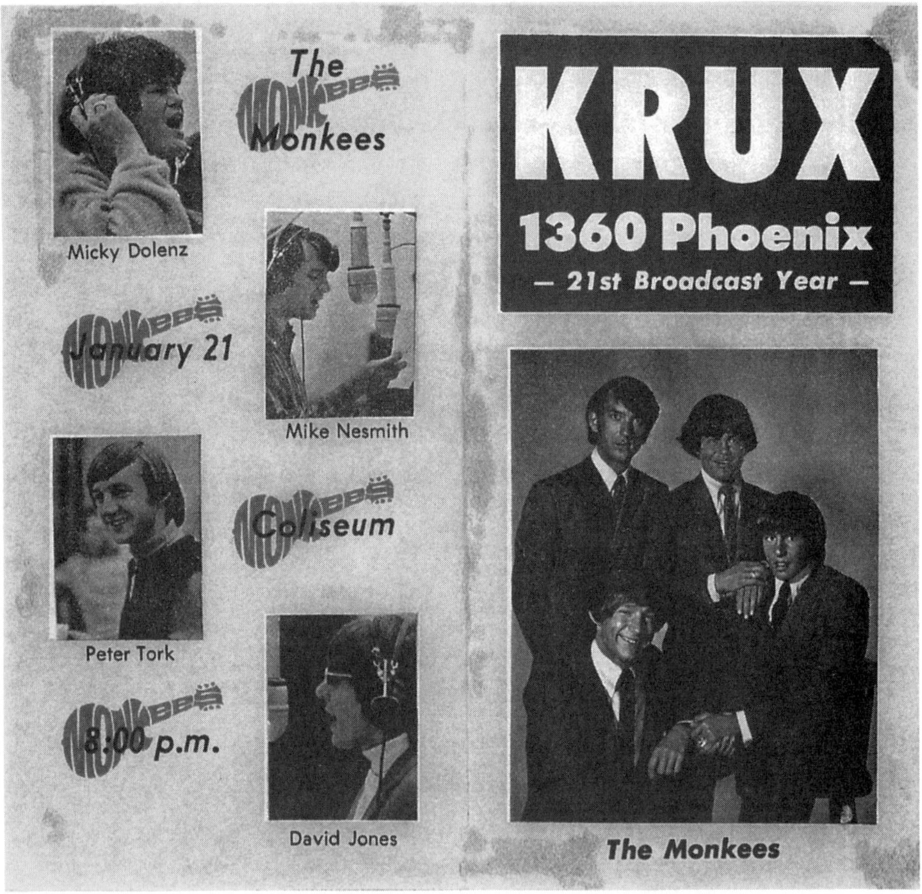
The Monkees
Micky Dolenz
January 21
Mike Nesmith
Coliseum
Peter Tork
8:00 p.m.
David Jones
KRUX
1360 Phoenix
— 21st Broadcast Year —
The Monkees

# The KRUX Hip Hitparade

**EFFECTIVE JANUARY 13, 1967 -- 4 P.M.**

| Last Week | This Week | Title | Artist | Wks. on Survey |
|---|---|---|---|---|
| ( 1) | 1. | I'M A BELIEVER/ I'M NOT YOUR STEPPIN' STONE | MONKEES | 9 |
| ( 2) | 2. | SNOOPY VS. THE RED BARON | ROYAL GUARDSMEN | 6 |
| ( 3) | 3. | WINCHESTER CATHEDRAL | NEW VAUDEVILLE BAND | 14 |
| ( 5) | 4. | BUT IT'S ALRIGHT | J. J. JACKSON | 6 |
| (11) | 5. | TELL IT LIKE IT IS | AARON NEVILLE | 5 |
| ( 6) | 6. | BORN FREE | MATT MONRO | 7 |
| ( 7) | 7. | SUGAR TOWN | NANCY SINATRA | 11 |
| (10) | 8. | FULL MEASURE/NASHVILLE CATS | LOVIN' SPOONFUL | 5 |
| ( 8) | 9. | EAST WEST | HERMAN'S HERMITS | 7 |
| (22) | 10. | 98.6 | KEITH | 3 |
| (12) | 11. | BLUE'S THEME | THE ARROWS | 6 |
| ( 9) | 12. | LADY GODIVA | PETER & GORDON | 11 |
| (13) | 13. | GOOD THING | PAUL REVERE & RAIDERS | 7 |
| (15) | 14. | SINGLE GIRL | SANDY POSEY | 10 |
| (16) | 15. | WHERE WILL THE WORDS COME FROM | GARY LEWIS | 5 |
| (17) | 16. | STANDING IN THE SHADOW OF LOVE | FOUR TOPS | 4 |
| ( 4) | 17. | THAT'S LIFE | FRANK SINATRA | 9 |
| (19) | 18. | COLOR MY WORLD | PETULA CLARK | 4 |
| (20) | 19. | KNOCK ON WOOD | EDDIE FLOYD | 5 |
| (25) | 20. | THERE'S GOT TO BE A WORD | INNOCENCE | 3 |
| (21) | 21. | MUSTANG SALLY | WILSON PICKETT | 3 |
| (23) | 22. | IT MAY BE WINTER OUTSIDE | FELICE TAYLOR | 4 |
| (30) | 23. | GEORGY GIRL | THE SEEKERS | 2 |
| (24) | 24. | HELP ME GIRL | ERIC BURTON & ANIMALS | 5 |
| (29) | 25. | I'VE PASSED THIS WAY BEFORE | JIMMY RUFFIN | 2 |
| (28) | 26. | KNIGHT IN RUSTY ARMOR | PETER & GORDON | 2 |
| (—) | 27. | WORDS OF LOVE | MAMAS & PAPAS | 1 |
| (HB) | 28. | RUBY TUESDAY | ROLLING STONES | 1 |
| (18) | 29. | PUSHIN' TOO HARD | THE SEEDS | 7 |
| (HB) | 30. | PRETTY BALLERINA | LEFT BANKE | 1 |

**HITBOUNDS**

| | | |
|---|---|---|
| | FOR WHAT IT'S WORTH | THE BUFFALO SPRINGFIELD |
| | LOOK WHAT YOU'VE DONE | POOZO SEGO SINGERS |
| | STAND BY ME | SPYDER TURNER |

LUCKY LAWRENCE 6-9

NORM SEELEY 9-12

DICK GRAY 12-3

KIT CARSON 3-7

BOB SHANNON 7-12

WILKERSON 12-6

Phoenix radio station, KRUX's 'Top 30' song list promoting the Monkees concert.

dad in the world?). I managed to push my way to the front of the group of people standing at the sidewalk entrance to where their rooms were. Nothing was happening. Everyone just stood there. Finally, I asked the girl next to me why no one just ran down the breezeway past the guard (there was only one!). She told me they had promised him they would be good and not try anything like that. Legal secretary in the making already has the wheels spinning in her head, 'I didn't make any such promise!' When the guard looked away, I took off running! I heard people yelling and heard footsteps chasing after me. I never looked back. I got through the breezeway, past the patios of the room and saw Micky standing by a palm tree. I stopped about 10 feet from him and just froze. At that point the security guard chasing me grabbed my arm, and Micky said, 'Leave her alone.' My hero! So the guard let go, and he walked back to his post. No one else came after me. All the other fans kept their promises to the security guard!

By then, a few people came up to Micky and I got his autograph. I turned around and saw a group of girls by one of the rooms. I was getting braver by the moment, so I walked on up. And there he was. Darling David Jones! Sitting outside his room, wearing a long sleeved, white shirt, with the sleeves rolled up. He was patiently signing autographs for everyone standing around. I could not hear a thing, my heart was pounding so hard. I had never been this close to any celebrity, much less someone I was so crazy about! The only thing I had the presence of mind to do was bring a handful of blank envelopes with me. It never occurred to me that I'd ever be in a place to get a photo of Davy Jones! As I think about it, I'm sure my dad was the one who had them in the car and handed them to me before he let me go on my adventure.

I just stood there, staring at the top of Davy's head. Handing him an envelope to sign every couple of minutes. I got his autograph three times that day. I finally found my voice and asked him if he would put 'To Karen' on it. He started out writing my name with a 'C' and I corrected him. He crossed it out, and rewrote 'To Karen, Love David Jones.' Did he wonder how everyone got envelopes for him to sign? Who knows. I probably stood there for a good 15 minutes or longer. Looking at the top of his head, and seeing the little strands of hair that stood up a little. I finally reached out, took hold of one of the hairs at the bottom, and broke off a piece! I don't think he felt that, because I had been holding the bottom. I knew I didn't want to just yank it out of his head. Other girls thought that was a good idea too, only they just started yanking at the hair! He finally got tired of that business and ran his hand over his head and said, 'Cut it out!'

I don't remember what happened after that. I don't remember if we were told to leave, or if I finally just decided I didn't want to wear out my welcome and left. I held onto that hair for the longest time. I was happy. I finally went back to the car and told my dad I was ready to go and showed him the hair and the 3 Davy autographs and the single Micky autograph. He laughed. I still have that hair in my scrapbook and the four autographed envelopes. I can't believe how long I held onto a single piece of hair, probably an inch long. Nowadays, I just think, I have Davy DNA in my house! When I got home from my adventure, I called my friend Marilyn and told her what had happened. Dead silence. She was MAD! I didn't ask her to come along! How selfish. It never occurred to me, and I still apologize to her to this day for that little gaff! She said she has since forgiven me."

**WILD RECEPTION** — This is part of a capacity crowd of 13,000 that watched the Monkees perform at Memorial Coliseum last night.

Arizona Republic concert review, photo and Karen's ticket stub.

# Coliseum Rocks to Monkee-Mania
## Hundreds of Fans Turned Away at Big Show

**By TROY IRVINE**

It was Monkee-mania to the hilt.

"Yea yea, We're the Monkees," sang America's answer to the Beatles, and when they hit the stage at the coliseum a capacity 13,000 nearly sucked in the walls with one mighty gasp. Fifty security guards patroled the aisles and braced for a rush at the stage that never came.

**HUNDREDS** who were turned away at the doors when all the tickets, priced $2.75 to $5, were sold waited at the rear exit just to catch a glimpse of Mike Nesmith, Mickey Dolenz, Peter Tork and Davey Jones.

Tiny and boyish Davey effervesced like seltzer water. His tambourine playing and singing antics produced a hysteria that brought dozens of miniskirts to tears. And when he sailed his mod cap into the audience, a riot for its posession almost ensued.

**THE CROWD** generated so much energy that the Salt River Project was there trying to harness it. It would have been a field day for cardiograph machines.

And the Monkees DID sing and play their own instruments, settling a controversy of whether their only talent is romping about on their show, "The Monkees," on NBC-TV.

Nesmith, the lead guitar player, had said in a recent Saturday Evening Post article, "Tell the world that we don't record our own music. But that's US they see on television."

**ASKED BEFORE** the show if the group was going to play and sing live, Nesmith said, "Stand up next to the amplifier. If you can hear us at all, you'll hear that we're playing."

He wasn't joking. Two Vox amps, 6 feet high, combined with six others were so loud that many of the security police stuffed cotton in their ears.

The show opened with the Candy Store Prophets, with Bobby Hart, a Phoenix lad, doing the lead singing and playing organ. Hart and partner Tommy Boyce have cowritten most of the Monkees' recordings, including the multimillion-selling "Last Train to Clarksville" and "I'm a Believer."

**THE MONKEES** didn't sound as full or polished as on their records but nonetheless dispelled any beliefs they are musially deficient. While they were performing the stage was bombarded with flashbulbs, candy, hair-brushes, paper cups and even a teddy bear.

When the Monkees left at the end of the show, two of their dummy limousines were sent out and submerged by hundreds of screaming teen-boppers. Meanwhile, they escaped out a side exit and made their getaway to Sky Harbor Airport, where their plane left the ground around 10:30 p.m.

```
E B  10   1
Sec.  Row  Seat
Ariz. Veterans Memorial Coliseum
SAT. JAN. 21, 1967
    8:00 P. M.
  ARENA FLOOR
```

(Editor's note: Here is my account of the concert).

A friend called me up one evening and asked me if I wanted to go to the Monkees concert with him. I said, "Sure," and it was planned. I guess I was the ripe old age of 19 by then, and still working at the bank. When we got there the place was packed! The Arizona State Coliseum, where the concert took place, is no small building, and it was filled to the rafters. We had seats on the side, not too far up. We discovered that the audience was mostly 14 year old girls. My friend and I kind of felt like old men there, but everyone was into seeing the Monkees, so there was a real common bond. We were getting a kick out of watching the girls screaming their lungs out, and the show hadn't even started yet!

Finally, a group called the Candy Store Prophets, headed by Bobby Hart, opened the show. I knew who he was from studying a song book of the Monkees I had bought some time before. He was one half of Boyce & Hart, the songwriting duo who penned many of the Monkees hits. I remember thinking to myself that this guy was talented and Hollywood slick. He had a tailor-made, cream-colored suit on and played a Vox, stand-up organ. I don't remember the songs they played, but they were about as good of a rock & roll band as you can get. Of course everybody was dying in their seats waiting for the Monkees. At last, the time had come, and the Monkees appeared. Boy, what a roar went up from the girls! The guys said hello's and hi's and thank you's through the noise and quickly went into their first number. The lights went down in the coliseum as the Monkees started playing. Then the explosions of hundreds of tiny, instamatic camera flashbulbs went off, and continued throughout the concert. You couldn't be in the place without feeling the charge of energy and electricity going through there like a lightning bolt.

The guys were putting on a very good, entertaining show while playing all their hits. Somewhere in the show Micky did 'Goin' Down.' He came running in from the side of the stage, did a somersault and launched into the song. He was fantastic! In one part they had a strobe light going as Micky did some incredible foot work, beating out James Brown and Mick Jagger. Then the format was changed and each of the Monkees did a solo spot with Bobby Hart and The Candy Store Prophets backing them up musically. Micky or one of the other Monkees introduced each of the solo spots. Mike did a real rocking and rolling number. Peter did his banjo. Micky did a great song and Davy did a song that I forget what it was, but it sounded like something from a Broadway show. I kept thinking that he really does have a good voice and that he must have been on Broadway before (I did not know at the time that he had been on Broadway). During Davy's song he had on a John Lennon type of cap. At the exact minute his song ended he took the cap and threw it out into the audience (another incredible roar). Later when I worked with Davy and his publishing partner, Alan Green, on their book 'Mutant Monkees' I asked Davy about this incident. Sorry, you'll have to read his reply to me about this a little further on in the book.

The Monkees did more numbers and before anyone knew it it was all over. I know everyone left, as we did, thinking that the Monkees are some great performers. It was a fun, exciting concert and experience. Of course, the girls may have had a bit of a different viewpoint, after all they had just seen their knights in shining armor.

## Alan Green, Davy Jones and a Book

In the summer of 1991 I had the opportunity to work with Alan Green and Davy Jones on a second book they were doing. The first book they did together was entitled 'They Made a Monkee Out of Me,' Davy's autobiography. Alan was Davy's musical director on his solo tours. Both of them came from Manchester, England. How my working with them came about started with a friend of mine. I had heard of the book 'They Made A Monkee Out of Me,' and I had heard that it was done by Davy and a partner, and that they had published it themselves. I wanted to see the book and see what they had done. I had an interest in it because I had just finished my first book, on Dennis Wilson (the late drummer of The Beach Boys), and I was just then finishing up a second book on Jim Morrison, of The Doors. My friend had a mailing address for Alan Green, who she said was the partner that worked with Davy on the first book.

Well, I sent Alan a copy of my book, which goes by the title of 'Denny Remembered, Dennis Wilson In Words and Pictures,' and a short letter explaining how this was my first book and that I would love to see their book. In a short time I got a nice letter back from Alan telling me how much he loved my book, and he had also sent me a copy of their book, signed by both Alan and Davy. Then a few days after that I got a telephone call from Alan and we had a long conversation. Another thing I had done in my Denny book was to include some photo/color designs that I do. I add color to black and white photo images using my own technique (without the use of a computer). Alan asked me about these and told me how much he loved my work. Then he told me about the second book that Davy and he were just starting. Alan asked me if he sent some Monkees photos, could I do my color design work to them. I told him I would be thrilled to do so. I also told him how much I was enjoying their book and we became a kind of mutual admiration society.

Alan started sending me some great Monkees photos to work on and I would send them back to him after doing my magic. I don't do my color design right on the original photos, but just use the photos to begin my design work. So I would return his original photos along with a color design, sometimes I would give him two, or three different color designs from the one photo. Anyway, Alan loved this stuff and wanted to use more for the new book. Before too long Alan asked me if I would like to come out to work with him and Davy for a week, or two. To me this was a great honor, and I told Alan that I would love to be able to work with him and Davy. Plans were made and before I knew it I was on a plane to join them.

When the plane touched down Alan was there to pick me up at the airport. Also, with him was a Monkee historian by the name of Fred Velez from New York City. Fred was a real nice, friendly guy who I carried on a conversation with as we made our way to Alan's house. The plan was for us to stop at Alan's house so I could drop off my bags, get freshened up a little and head over to Davy's house, where Davy was rehearsing his band at that very moment. Alan had a

Davy's kitchen bulletin board with his tour dates posted.

beautiful old farm house, in which parts of the construction of the house was over 175 years old. Alan was anxious to see more photo color/designs that I had brought with me. He wanted to take them over to Davy's. I had also brought two copies of my second book, which had just come off the press, on Jim Morrison. I had already signed one to Alan, and one to Davy.

Soon Alan was driving us over to Davy's, which was only a few miles away. I have to admit that I was a little nervous about meeting Davy. We got to Davy's big, 3-story, turn-of-the-century home and went in through the back which led into the kitchen. Davy and his band was taking a break from rehearsal. Introductions were made and Davy gave me a soft drink from the refrigerator. I gave Davy the copy of my Jim Morrison book, and showed him the color designs. Alan was watching us with what I thought was curiosity as to how Davy and I would hit it off. I think there was some sort of rite of passage going on between Davy and myself. I didn't know what I had to do to pass. Alan showed Davy one of my designs that I had done of Davy and his family when he was very young. He just stood there silently looking at it with no show of emotion. I thought to myself that if this was some kind of test, I wish it would get over with. I didn't know if Davy reacted this way to all newcomers, or if he had to know someone for a period of time before he let down his defenses, and gave out some trust and friendship. I didn't want to dwell on it and thought it best to let it ride. Perhaps, as time went on, things would become a little better. Soon, Davy and his band went back into the living room to rehearse and Alan, Fred and I went outside and just hung out. As the day wore on and started turning into sunset Alan came from the house and informed Fred and myself that all of us were going out to dinner, everyone, including Davy

Davy's set list for rehearsal.

and the band. We had a convoy of vehicles going down the country road headed to a roadside café that Davy knew of. Reservations had been made and when we arrived they were expecting us. We went into a private section of the dinner house and helped pull together two huge wood tables to accommodate our motely group of musicians, writers, artists and a Monkee. Davy sat at the head of the table, as a King holding forth his Court. We sort of looked like The Last Supper. Conversation became lively as the Knights and their King told jokes, with Davy always surpassing everyone else with his punchlines. I was getting a little punchy from my long day and the long flight. We had a wonderful dinner, which Davy paid for, and then he announced that we would all go to a neighborhood bar down the road, "for a drink." I figured maybe my first day there wasn't over yet.

As we walked outside and were heading towards the cars a family was looking at us, as they were heading inside. They stopped and said some things to each other, of which "Davy Jones" was the only thing I could pick up. Davy stopped, so everyone else stopped as we looked at the family. I knew this whole thing was not hostile, but it sure was different. Finally, Davy said a hello to them and some other kind remarks. The family was still on the steps of the roadhouse looking at us when we drove off in our cars. If this was how things were, I could imagine what it would be like when we stopped at the local bar "for a drink."

As soon as we went into the bar I noticed people looking and they continued to look. I also noticed people at tables 'elbow' their companions. At least there wasn't a mob of people who rushed up to Davy and started pulling his hair and clothes. Our group kind of floated around the place, everybody finding spots to

Alan Green in Davy's living room.

sit down, or to continue mingling. I talked with Alan and Fred and a couple of guys in the band. Davy was just standing over by me so I tried to strike up a conversation. He was pleasant enough and I thought that maybe the ice was breaking a little. He asked if I wanted a drink and I said I would, just a Coke. At that time I wasn't drinking. When he was waiting for my drink he had some money folded with a clip on it. He had a pen and was tapping it on the money clip saying, "Please multiply, please multiply." We talked more as we stood by the bar and I told him of the Monkees concert I saw in Phoenix, Arizona in January of 1967. I reminded him of when he had finished a song and he had tossed his cap out into the audience. He turned to me and said, "Yeah, I shouldn't have done that. I had my car keys in it." It was fun standing there shooting the breeze with Davy Jones. I never thought when I use to watch the Monkees TV show that someday I would be standing next to Davy having a conversation, let alone doing artwork for a book of his.

As the evening wore on, with Alan coming around again and again to talk, I noticed that he and everone else was getting progressively more smashed. Fred wasn't drinking either and we both wondered what the evening held, and what we had gotten ourselves into. This was a Saturday night, who knew what evil lurked out there. Only the Shadow knew! Pretty soon the bar was closing and everybody had to head out. As we were going to the cars I saw a little red sportscar driving round and round in circles. There were two blonds in it, and two of the guys from the band were chasing the car. They finally got close to it and both of them dove into the back of the little car. The car with the two blonds and the two members of the band, legs hanging out of the back, sped off into the darkness of the night, and we didn't see them again for two days.

What was left of our gang headed back to Davy's house. It was a warm night and we all hung out on Davy's back porch. Alan and Davy strolled over to some of the gigantic trees that surrounded the property there and carried on a loud, animated conversation. The reader has to remember that these two Englishmen were from the same hometown of Manchester and they really had their own way of talking, their own brand of humor and their own way of communicating with each other that was something that outsiders like us could not understand. It was fun to watch and listen to, but most of the time I didn't have a clue what they were talking about. And both of them were fast! Talk about sharp wits! They had them, you couldn't top them in jokes, or one-liners. You could give that idea up.

I was totally worn out and finally Alan decided to go home so Fred and I could get some sleep. Dawn was not far off. We pulled up to Alan's country home and went inside. Fred went to his room right away to retire and Alan started playing his piano. I had never heard Alan play before so I sat down in a chair by him. He was completely caught up in the music and played some fantastic things. Later, he would tape an album for me that he had done a few years back, when he was signed to a record label. Alan was a gifted songwriter as well and I thought he was the perfect match as Davy's musical director. I finally made my way upstairs to my room as the first rays of morning light started to filter through. I was worn out mentally and physically from this first day and really hoped that the other days wouldn't be like this, and I could get down to some work. My hopes and wishes were fulfilled because we then started on the task at hand.

The first thing we did was to go over to Davy's house and start bringing over Davy's collection of memorabilia to sort through for the book. We ended up with about 8 huge boxes of stuff. And I mean large, moving type of boxes. Alan told me that when Davy was working on the TV series he would go out to the dumpsters every evening and see what the crew had thrown away that day. They would throw out photographs, contact sheets and all kinds of incredible things that Davy would save. That was just a small part of what was in these boxes. We started making piles of things by topic in Alan's den, which soon spread into his living room and then hallway. We could hardly work around. There was a pile of photos of Davy with other celebrities, a stack of scrapbooks given to him by fans (and these were thick scrapbooks filled with good material), Monkee bubble gum cards, tons of Teen Magazines like 16, Tiger Beat, etc., tons of photos, contact sheets, snapshots taken by the Monkees themselves, letters, contracts, promotional materials, cards, and on and on.

My main job was really just as a contributor to the book with my color designs, but I helped out in any other ways that I could, and enjoyed every minute of it. I did play with Alan's computer a little, taking a couple photos and seeing what I could do with them by adding color, but my main way of doing that was with my own method. I did not help in decision making in regards to what would go in the book, that was all up to Davy and Alan. However, my color designs were the first ones Alan had, and then he got the brainstorm to start talking to computer/graphic artists about using their work.

This brings the story up to the point of, what really did happen to the book? For those who remember the unfolding of events, and those who had pre-ordered the book I hope this information sheds some light on the unfortunate things that later took place. For those who don't know the story, in a nutshell Alan

L. to R.   Davy's brother-in-law, Rita (Alan Green's
          Girlfriend), Davy Jones (at Alan's house).

advertised that those who ordered the book early would get a discount on the price. The early orders would go to the costs of printing the book. The problem was that nobody got the book. At first, Alan was going to have the book in black and white, then when he decided to use my color designs there was going to be some color pages. But Alan started going with the philosophy of 'more is better' and started talking to all these computer/graphic artists, which also greatly delayed the book. Soon, the black and white book became a totally full-color book, and a very costly and expensive book to produce.

Alan is an honest person and a incredible talent, he never intended to mislead or rip anyone off, but he made some bad judgements and got in over his head. After I had worked with Alan and Davy and came back home I would get updates in the mail about the book (just like everybody else). The updates would say that there was this, or that delay and thanking everyone for their patience. I talked to Alan on the phone and told him that these 'improvements' he was doing on the book were not good because he had gone way over his delivery date. I said, "Alan, just wrap it up and send it to the people," but he had different reasons for going the way he was. Later, I couldn't even get through on his phone, it was a 'leave a message,' recording, or some such thing. I was getting worried because I knew this could be a big problem brewing.

There were problems now between Alan and Davy. Alan eventually sent me a hardcover and softcover edition of the book and a letter. He said that he had gone bankrupt and that the bank came and took all of the books against unpaid bills. It was very bad news to hear. Alan went on cruise ships as an entertainer, and it was not a very happy time for him. Just recently I saw a copy of 'Mutant Monkees' in a major bookstore chain. I wondered how that could be, and did some research on the InterNet. I discovered there were copies of it out there and when I started doing this book I learned that fans had copies of it too. I do not know how it was settled, if Davy got the books from the bank, or if there was a second print run, but I was happy that the work on the book wasn't in vain and it did get circulated. And that is the story of Alan Green, Davy Jones and a Book.

Davy's Union Jack in his study room window.

Micky looking good in concert.

### How To Touch A Monkee

This next section is all by Joanna Parsons and her very funny and hilarious account of her experiences with each of the individual Monkees. The crazy humor of it all just made me laugh out loud when I first read it. I'm sure it will do the same for you. I'll start it off with the tamer encounters and go from there.

\* "We went to NYC on January 29, 1999 for Mike Nesmith's book signing. I was very excited because Mike was the only Monkee I had not met in person, or gotten an autograph from, or a picture with. As usual, we were there five hours before Nez was due to arrive. As we were waiting, someone from the bookstore told us that Mike would only be signing his book and nothing else. I was loaded with other stuff, so that was disappointing. She also said that there would be no posed pictures, but we could take as many other pictures as we wanted. When it was my turn Mike signed my book. He was nice and talked to everyone. While he was signing my book...I was looking at him...and I had to touch him. So I reached out and started rubbing his shoulder while he was writing. He smiled and handed me back my book and said, 'Thanks, and you have a great day.' I hope to see Mike again in the future. I want a real hug and a nice posed pic.

Mike Nesmith at booksigning.

* On May 23, 1998 we went to the Freelance Human Being Party in Morristown, NJ to see Peter Tork. The show was great. Between sets Peter mingled with everyone and signed some autographs, but he didn't pose for any pictures. After the show I went up to him and asked if he would pose for a picture with me. He said, 'I really can't. We're running late and we were suppose to be out of this room by now. I still have to pack up all of my equipment.' There was no way I was going to take no for an answer, so I said, 'Oh, ok, I understand. I'll help you pack up your stuff. I never did this before, but if you talk me through it, I'm sure I'll figure it out.' He looked at me and said, 'Go get your camera !!' When my husband snapped the photo I held Peter as close to me as possible. Peter also gave me the song list that he used that night. He gave everyone, who wanted one, a hug. His hugs are wonderful !! He bear-hugs you, and holds you close and tight. No wonder we all call him 'The Giver of Great Hugs !!'

* My husband, Geoff, and I went to see Davy, and his band at a small club in Pennsauken, NJ. This was before the Internet was popular (about 1990), and there was hardly anybody there! That was great for us, but not for Davy, I suppose. Anyway, there were two shows and we stayed for both. After the second show we were starting to leave. You had to walk through the bar area, and then through a foyer to go outside. As we were walking through the foyer, out of the corner of my eye, I saw the blue outfit that Davy was wearing onstage. I looked over, and there he was!!! All by himself, leaning in the side doorway, just staring into space. I grabbed my husband by the sleeve and started pulling him over to the doorway. He saw Davy and knew why I was pulling on him. I told my husband, 'Keep him there, and talking as long as you can.' We went up to Davy and said hi. He was

Joanna Parsons with Davy Jones.

real pleasant and talked with us. Finally, I couldn't stand it anymore and said, 'Do you mind if I touch you?' He put both arms in the air and said, 'Help yourself.' So while I'm running my hands up and down Davy, my husband is saying things like, 'So, you have a new album coming out soon?' (Don't worry Ed, I didn't touch anything too personal ... couldn't, after all, Geoff was standing right there and his sense of humor only stretches so far). After I groped him for a few minutes his limo arrived to take him home.

* The first time I met Micky Dolenz was at Mt. Airy Lodge in the Poconos of PA. The date was November 29, 1997. My husband, Geoff, my friend Phyllis and myself went to the show. We had a great time as usual. After the show we went to the bar in the lodge. We had heard that the guys would sometimes hang out there after the show. We entered and found a table near the bar. The room, of course, was packed. We looked over and there was Micky at the bar, drinking a beer. We snapped a few pics from our table, but we were trying very hard not to be obvious. A few minutes later Davy Jones came in and joined Micky at the bar. Now we were really getting psyched!! We took more pictures of the two of them together. It was getting late and I knew that the bar was going to close soon. I wanted to get a picture of Micky and myself, but he looked like he was just trying to relax and hang out, and I didn't want to be a bother. But, how many times do you find yourself in the same room with Micky Dolenz? I figured, why not? I'll ask him to pose for a pic. If he says no, what was the worst that could happen, besides me falling to the floor, sobbing? I told my friend Phyllis, 'Get the camera ready, I'm going for it.' I walked over to him and I said, 'Excuse me, I know you are on your own time, and I don't mean to be a pest, but would you please pose for a picture with me?' I really expected him to say no. What

a pleasant surprise it was when he said, 'Sure, I would love to.' I stood next to him at the bar, so Phyllis could take the photo, but then Micky said, 'Let's go out to the lobby, there is more room there, the picture will be better.' All right!! We started walking out when suddenly he turned to me and said, 'Stop pushing me !' I said, 'I didn't push you, why would I push you, you're walking right beside me?' He said, 'I don't like it when people push me, so stop pushing me!' At this point, I was getting angry (Yes, Ed, we had ALL had a few drinks by now) and I said, 'Look, I didn't push you. The room is full of people, someone else may have pushed you. My hands have been at my side the whole time. I never touched you!" By now we were out in the lobby. Micky said, 'I don't care if you touch me…just don't push me!' I started laughing and said, 'Ok, you don't care if I touch you?….Take this!!' I grabbed him around the waist and pulled him close to me and started rubbing his stomach. He started laughing too, and Phyllis snapped the photo. Afterwards my husband told me he was starting to worry. He could see that I was mad and he thought Micky and I were going to brawl right then andthere!"

Joanna Parsons with Micky Dolenz.

Recent Peter Tork.

Recent Micky Dolenz

### Monkees Good Deeds

The Monkees really do have a heart, and these stories show it beyond a shadow of a doubt. I regret that I don't have more stories, but it's not from a lack of them, I just do not have access to them at this time. There are some good deed stories that are a part of the 'Fans' section, but I didn't want to pull them out, to place them here. It's good to know that our idols are 'real' people, and 'nice' people at that! Here's to The Golden Rule, and the Boy Scouts.......

*

In Davy and Alan Green's book 'They Made A Monkee Out of Me' Davy relates a story about how one day he got a call from a doctor at a hospital in Phoenix, Arizona. The doctor told him about two young girls who were carrying Monkees albums when they crossed a busy street and got run over. Davy said that one of the girls had very bad leg damage, and the other girl had been unconscious for six weeks. Of course, the doctor was hoping that Davy could come out and visit them, especially since the one girl was now coming out of her coma. The girls were starting to play their Monkees albums in the hospital and the doctor knew that a visit from Davy could restore their emotions, and even help in the recovery process. Davy agreed to come right away if the doctor promised not to alert the press, which he did.

Davy wrote in his book, "You should have seen their faces. Now I know how Santa Claus feels. You can't measure moments like that. If I'd had to fly twice around the world, it would've been worth it." Both of the girls lived on the same street in Phoenix, so they were neighborhood friends. Pictures were taken with Davy at the hospital and the family of both girls invited Davy home to dinner after they were able to leave the hospital. Davy later flew out to see them again, and through a terrible tragedy the two girls got to meet Davy Jones, and have happiness in their lives after all.

*

Another good deed by Mike Nesmith, along with the Other Monkees, was recorded in the book 'Total Control, The Michael Nesmith Story' by Randi L. Massingill.

Mike helped organize producer Chip Douglas, recording engineer Hank Cicalo, the other Monkees and everything else that needed to be done so that they could create what was to be the Monkees first album, completely done by them from start to finish. All the songs were to be written by them, and all the instruments were to be played by the Monkees. The album was called 'Headquarters' and they were very proud of it.

In 'Total Control' Hank Cicalo was quoted as saying that he was getting a lot of pressure from the powers that be to come in on time with the album. Cicalo was telling the guys to quit fooling around, that they had to finish the album. "I kept telling the guys 'There's no more time. We don't have any more time. There's no time. No time." He said that the reason he was saying that is because the guys kept saying that they would go home and get another song done. But he was saying that there was no time for that.

Cicalo said he started screaming that there was no time for two days until the Monkees realized that there really was something wrong. Michael was quoted in the book as saying to Cicalo, "Give us a couple minutes…" The guys were gone for about an hour and when they came back in Chip Douglas started work on it with the guys. The end result was the song 'No Time.' It's recorded that the Monkees were doing vocals and Cicalo "leaned over and (I) gave them a couple of lines for the song." And of course, he had been the inspiration for the title, and the song itself.

The song was soon mixed, and everyone was happy with it. Lester came to check out the album, and along with the four Monkees everyone agreed that they had done it. The group went up to Hank Cicalo, "and they said 'Hank, thanks a lot. That's your song.' I said 'What? Michael said, 'That's your song.' He said, 'For all the time over the last year and a half, you've really been great for us and stuck it all out and all the craziness and we wanted to give you something. Here's a song.'"

In 'Total Control' Cicalo asked if anyone knew what a Monkees song is worth and he went on to explain that he bought a house for $50,000 with the money, and that the house today is worth between $250,000-$300,000. And Cicalo was quoted as saying, "And I owe that to them and I owe that to Michael for doing that. That was one of the nicest things that anybody ever did for me."

*

"My daughter, Katherine, or Katie, who is now 7 years of age, has come to know and love the old sitcom favorites of the 50's, 60's and 70's thanks to Nickelodeon, and its companion channel TV Land. One evening without warning I heard a familiar tune. As I drew near to the television, there, on Nick At Nite, was that zany, old show 'The Monkees.' It was as though time had stood still. As my daughter and I watched, it was like a stroll down memory lane for me, remembering the 'Teen Idol' days of my youth, and those magazines like Tiger Beat, with all the heart-throbs...especially Davy Jones! Children adore harmless fun, and Katie is no exception. She honed right in on the slapstick antics that captured the childhood innocence of the Monkees. Katie continued to watch the show, enjoying it every time. There was even a marathon of shows all evening.

Then it was announced that the Monkees tour would be coming to the Bloomsburg Fair, in Bloomsburg, Pennsylvania. I was anxious to see the show, and Katie asked if she could tag along as she was caught up in the hype of the TV series. After the show at the fair, the crush began for Davy Jones. While at such a young age, I was not certain that she could distinguish the television show from the show at the fair, but Davy's boyish looks captivated her. It seemed like it was Tiger Beat days all over again! We then heard a radio advertisement that Davy would be performing at the Front Street Station in Northumberland, PA. Katie was ecstatic and asked if we could go to his show. Little did I know what an impact he would eventually have on my daughter's life.

Through different sources, we had heard of Davy's love for animals; in particular, horses. Katie has a menagerie of pets of her own, one being her Shetland pony, Cochise. The day before Davy was to appear at the Front Street Station, Katie took a spill while riding her pony. She was more scared than hurt, but was emphatic that she did not want to ride

Cochise again. The next day we went to see Davy. At the end of his performance we stood in line to speak with him, and obtain his autograph. Katie was so excited! As we approached him, his greeting to her was, 'ello, pretty girl!' in that British accent. She told him about Cochise, and he encouraged her not to give up, but to keep riding. Those words impacted her greatly, and had her counting the hours till the next morning when she could get back on her pony. And she has been riding ever since. Later, Katie sent him a letter, telling him how much she enjoyed the show, and thanking him for all his kindness. To our surprise, several days afterwards, she received an autographed picture of David standing in the barn with his horse!"

*

"My name is Kathy and I became a huge Monkees fan, in particular of Davy, who I had a big crush on. He's still my favorite Monkee. I wrote him a letter a few years ago, as we appeared to share interests – he had his stud and was writing a book, and I have horses and was also writing a book. He telephoned my house to speak with me as a result, but I was on holiday – he never called back! (Editor's note: Davy if you are reading this, call Kathy). To this day I get excited when I hear a Monkees song on the radio and love listening to their music. I also saw all 4 of them in 1997, which was a dream come true!"

*

"Back in 1994, my husband, myself, my mother-in-law and all four of our young children were poisoned by an old furnace leaking carbon monoxide. It nearly killed us. We were sick constantly. After the furnace was discovered, permanent neurological and brain damage had occurred in two of our children, my husband, myself and mother-in-law from the toxic gas and lack of oxygen to the brain.

For the next four years, we took ourselves and our children to over 50 doctors, trying to find out the extent of the damage, and possible treatments for the carbon monoxide poisoning. The two affected children became almost impossible to handle, developed behaviour problems they were unable to control, and started failing school. They could not, and still can't, maintain concentration in class, and have extreme difficulties retaining information.

The last year has been torture for our family, and it had left us near bankruptcy. One thing, though, that would always calm the kids and put a smile on everyone's face, was playing anything by the Monkees. See, I've been a David Jones and Monkees fan for 30 years. My four little Monkeenauts adore David and the Monkees. So when we heard that David Jones was appearing in Syracuse, NY at the State Fair for the Teen Idols Tour, my husband and I agreed that we would travel the 170 miles round trip just to see him, and let the kids have one tiny enjoyment.

A few days before we went, the sweet woman that runs David's official page forwarded a signing we did of his guestbook, telling about our medical and financial problems and our determination to meet him. David found out about it, and invited us, to come backstage to meet him personally as soon as we could get there. NEVER have my kids been so excited. We sang Monkees songs the whole 80 mile drive. Then came the biggest thrill in my family's life! We were invited into a private area to meet David. He was warm and loving. He hugged all my kids, posed for pictures, even letting my little one take his picture by stooping down for him. He even planted a kiss on my cheek – the one man whose music and talent I had adored for over 30 years! Oh my God, were the kids thrilled! They love him almost as much as I do. We had such a wonderful ride back to the house, it brought tears to my eyes.

Even now the children still enjoy telling everyone in their class how they met David Jones. One act of kindness from a wonderful performer for his fans has made it much easier for us to bear our hardships. We will always be grateful to this sweet, caring performer who put his fans' prioritys first."

Micky's first 'Teen Idol Tour' autograph tent, Georgia Dome 5-15-99, Atlanta, GA.

Davy in action at the 'Teen Idol Tour' Frederick Brown Jr. Amphitheater 8-22-98, Peachtree City, GA.

## Abby Alterio's Story About A Special Friend

As mentioned earlier in the book, Abby Alterio runs the official Davy Devotees fan club website authorized by Davy Jones himself. The website is located at:www.geocities.com/davydevotee/dd2.html The following story is very touching and also very heart wrenching, concerning someone who was very special to Abby. This is a sad story, but it is also inspiring in its own way. It shows that there is a place for kindness and goodness, and that dreams can come true in this life, as well as in the life to come. It shows that what we do is important to others, and that an act of kindness continues on, even after we are gone. I hope this story inspires the reader to look for opportunities to help others, and to discover what the most important things are in life.

"In November 1995, Peter Tork made an appearance at an Indianapolis Ice IHL hockey game. Having lived in Indianapolis all my life, and never having met a Monkee before, I was thrilled! At that time I had no fan club yet and the InterNet wasn't something I was very familiar with, though I had just gotten an online service with e-mail. I went to the hockey game, met Peter and saw his concert afterwards. A few days after, I got online and posted a message on the bulletin boards on Prodigy's service, that I had gone to Peter's show that night, and how much I enjoyed meeting him.  A lady by the name of Elicia LaCroix e-mailed me and said she had also been at the game to see Peter and that she had photos from the concert.  I was really excited about that, having never had any contact with another Monkees fan before.  So, she offered to send me the photos, telling me she had been published in Monkee Business Fanzine quite a bit due to her amount of concert going, etc.

It turned out that Elicia lived in South Bend, IN which is in the far northern portion of the state.  I was even more excited to learn she lived in my home state regardless of the distance from Indianapolis to South Bend.  As we became e-mail pals, I learned that Elicia's name was really Mary Powell.  She used a pen name online and in the fanzine to remain anonymous.  It never occurred to me why this would be important, so I took her explanation in stride and never questioned her about it.  As time went by, we started talking with each other on the phone.  Mary sort of took me under her wing, I guess, and I'll never know exactly why she 'chose' me, but she did.  She was about my mom's age and had a son roughly a year older than me.  She was married and had a great family life.

The Monkees' 30th anniversary was coming up in 1996 and I was elated to learn that the guys were going to have concerts again.  This was my chance to finally see one! They were to perform in Cincinnati, OH at the zoo there, in July of 1996.  I was fortunate enough to have a good friend who tolerated my fascination with the Monkees and drove me to the show (at 17, my parents were not going to allow me to go alone, or drive by myself).  Earlier that year, I had started Davy Devotees, and spoke with Mary about how badly I wanted to meet Davy, and how I knew it was never going to happen because he wouldn't make a trip to Indianapolis, and I could not travel by myself to see him. Mary kept telling me not to give up, and to believe in my dream. She told me that I never knew what would happen, and to have faith.

Mary and I had made tentative plans to meet up at the show in Cincinnati. I really wanted to finally meet her in person. But, something happened and she couldn't make the show. A few months prior to the concert, she started sharing more 'insider' information about the Monkees and her connection to them with me. She had been following them for a few years, having met Peter, in particular, several times. In fact, I believe he pretty much knew her by name, if not just by sight. I can't recollect exactly what her relationship was with the other members of the group (mostly Peter and Micky), but I think she may have been a casual friend of both of theirs. I thought this was awesome! Of course to me this seemed like a whole different world since I had never known anyone with her type of background before. Mary shared bits of her life with me on the phone as time went on. I think it was in May of 1996 that we became aware of a Monkees concert in Merrillville, IN (which was very close to South Bend, where Mary lived).

As soon as my parents gave me permission to attend this concert and the one in Cincinnati, I instantly called Mary. At this point, I was more excited at the idea of getting to see Mary in person than attending 2 concerts in one month. Mary told me she really thought she could make this show! On top of that, she finally told me one final important aspect of her life. She was best friends with a lady who was dating Micky Dolenz (I won't mention her name, to protect her identity, but she is legitimate). This lady lived in Florida and Mary was almost positive she would come up to Indiana for this concert. I was overwhelmed at the thought of finally meeting Mary and the girlfriend of a Monkee! As August 16th got closer, Mary called and confirmed that this lady would be at the concert. They purchased tickets and plans were made.

On the night of August 14th, I received a phone call from Mary, saying she had a surprise for me. She said someone wanted to talk to me and she put Micky's girlfriend on the phone. She introduced herself and told me, "I spoke with Micky and he has reserved 3 backstage passes for you and your friend for the show." I instantly flipped out. I don't know how many times I thanked her that night. Mary was put back on the phone and she said something like, "Didn't I tell you not to worry about meeting Davy? I can't begin to tell how thrilled I was. Mary was so happy for me, she kept laughing and saying, "Isn't it exciting?" It seemed to be as fun for her to hear my reaction, as it was for me at the thought of meeting Davy. That's the type of person Mary was. We made plans to meet at Mary's hotel room a few hours before the concert in 2 days.

I also had plans to meet some Internet friends at a Denny's restaurant before that same concert, so this was going to be one heck of a day for me! When my friend and I got to Merrillville and checked into our own room, I instantly called to Mary's hotel which was just down the strip. She wasn't in yet, but they took a message from me to have her call me. We waited and waited and finally decided to go to her hotel. As I got there, I saw some people in Monkees t-shirts (I was wearing mine with Davy's photo on the front) and some of them stopped me, asking about my shirt. That was kind of fun. Upon getting to the check-in desk at Mary's hotel, I learned that she was in her room now! We rushed up there and knocked on the door. She knew it was me before she opened the door because she called my name. We hugged each other and it really did feel like seeing a long lost friend.

It turned out that she never did get my phone message, which is why she didn't call me back. I was so giddy, and Mary was so loving towards me. She was as genuine in person as she was on the phone. She told me that Micky's room was just a few doors down, and that his girlfriend should be coming any second. When she came in, I started thanking her all over again, and both of them seemed so enlightened by my innocence and gratitude. Micky's girlfriend had some pictures of her with him, and she shared some nice stories about him with my friend and I. She and Mary shared some inside jokes, and the atmosphere was so nice. I didn't get to spend much time with them because of the fateful Internet gathering I had promised to attend, but, at least, I did get to spend a bit of time talking with Mary. They didn't really shoo me away, but they seemed to have some plans too. We agreed to meet up later after they had gotten the passes from the box office, which is where Micky said they would be waiting. I was to run back to their room after the Internet gathering and get the passes.

So, I went to the Internet gathering and met Joe whom I talked to for so long that I was running late for my second meeting with Mary!! We had to hurry and exchange phone numbers so that my friend and I could run back to the hotel room. My friend got to the room first because I had to search for a parking place and when I got up there, Mary suddenly opened the door, Micky's girlfriend was looking very disappointed. I said, "What happened?" and Mary said, "We tried and tried, but the lady at the box office couldn't give us the passes. I'm so sorry." I was so completely disappointed, I started bawling right there! That was my one and only chance to meet Davy. Mary quickly rushed to me and gave me a hug and said, "No!! I'm just kidding! Don't cry. We have the passes!" Micky's girlfriend hurriedly gave them to me. Mary felt so bad for putting me through that, but she was so fast to comfort me. My friend said to Micky's girlfriend, "See, I told you not to do that." I think at that moment Mary saw just how special she was to me, for doing that. I know she understoodhow much all this meant to me, but I don't know that it registered with her until then that it was so special.

We made plans to meet in Indianapolis and possibily travel together to see more shows. I had to rush out because the concert was to start in about an hour or so. When we got to the concert, we ran into Mary again, and she gave us her tickets (which were center stage a few rows back) because Micky had upgraded her seats for them. After the show, we ran into Mary and her pal in the hallway, looking for the 'backstage train' (as it was called), that was to contain people with backstage passes. I hung onto Mary for dear life as we fought through the crowd to make our way backstage. When we got backstage, she and her friend stayed off to the side, just observing the surroundings, talking with each other. I could tell this was 'old hat' for her, and that this whole backstage thing didn't need to happen because she would have hung out with Micky regardless, meaning it was that much more special that she went to the trouble to get little old me back there. Micky came out first, followed by Peter, and then Davy (who was the only one who was swamped by the crowd). When Davy came out and over to where I was standing, I looked over at Mary who was absolutely glowing and she mouthed, "You're welcome." That was the last time I saw her.

Mary and her friend made a very discreet exit as Micky left. I had no doubt in my mind, I'd hear from Mary in a few days because she was going to follow the tour to a few more cities, and then would return home. She had planned on going to Moline, IL the next day.

When I arrived home the next day my dad told me that he had received a phone call about Mary. My parents were well aware of who Mary was and what she had done for me. My dad sat me down and said that he had received a call from a club owner in Illinois, who owned the place where the Monkees were going to perform (in Moline, IL). The club owner told my dad that he knew that I was very important to Mary, and that he should contact me to let me know that Mary had a brain aneurysm the day after the concert in Merrillville, and that she was in a coma in an Illinois hospital. He said that it didn't look good, but she would be flown back to South Bend to be placed in a hospital in her hometown soon. I remember falling to the floor when I heard the news. I had never experienced a death in my family, or amongst any close friends before. I had never met anyone like Mary before, either. At this point, I learned that I meant as much to Mary as she did to me. My mom ran to me and held me as I cried and I went straight online, posting on the bulletin boards again that Mary was sick, and for fans to please pray for her. There was an instantaneous outpouring of love and friendship to me and others who knew Mary and I didn't even know they knew her, after this post online. It seemed that everyone who was 'someone' in Monkeedom knew of Mary, or knew her. It turned out, she was very well known, which is why she used a pen name online. Many people knew she had such good connections to the Monkees, so she was extremely cautious about who she chose as a friend, and who she shared portions of her life with. As her condition in the coma remained, the club owner called again (while I was out of the house) and told my dad that Mary had spoken about me the day after the concert and how happy she was to make my dream come true that night. He said that I meant a lot to Mary and to keep praying for her.

In September, she was taken off of life support, and she quietly died in a hospital in South Bend, IN. Mary lived just long enough to make my dream come true. Her husband, whom I had never spoken to, or heard from before sent me an e-mail shortly after her death, telling me how much I meant to her and how good a friend I was to her. I was so touched that I didn't know how to reply and felt such a complete and total sadness, as if a part of me was now missing. I still say, to this day, that I would gladly give back that meeting with Davy if I could just have my friend back. It is very overwhelming to me to have seen the tremendous outpouring of love from these Monkees fans online who were sending me, of all people, e-mails about Mary and how nice she was, and that I must have been very special to her. I never knew Mary was so 'famous,' nor did I have a clue that she cared so much about me. She never had a daughter, and I think that's how she saw me.

I dedicated the September 1996 edition of my newsletter to Mary – it held the full account of my meeting her and Davy, as well as the pictures I had taken with Davy, that to this day I dedicate to Mary. For a long time I had that picture on my webpage with the caption, 'Dedicated to Mary Powell, friend and fellow Monkee lover. See you in heaven.' But I just recently took it down and am going to place it somewhere else. I make a note to mention this story to as many people as I can because I want them to know there are good people in this world who don't expect anything in return for good deeds besides a warm smile. I have such vivid pictures in my mind of Mary and that night that I will never forget until the day I die. I will always remember her as the last time I saw her, mouthing, 'You're welcome' to me as I stood right next to Davy. Now, whenever someone contacts me who is a fan of Davy, or the Monkees and they keep telling me they'll 'never' meet the guys, I tell them to have faith and not to give up. This goes beyond just meeting the Monkees, these are words to live by in every aspect of life. Don't give up your dreams.

She was such a huge inspiration to me and my life, beyond the Monkees. I believe in angels and I feel everyone has an angel in their life at one point. Mary was my angel and I think that even the most faithless people have to believe in some religious factors within this story because she basically died right after I met her. She lived just long enough to fulfill a dream I had. My one regret is I didn't get a photograph of her, or spend a lot of time with her in her room, but I realize by not spending so much time with her I got to meet Joe, so something incredibly wonderful came out of this, and I just wish that I could share this happiness with Mary."

Peter at rehearsal.

Micky, with flowers.

## Photo Credits

Collection of Charlyne Smith: Page 15,17,19,20,21, 74 bottom, 75 both photos.

Collection of Vanessa Evans: Page 47,79.

Photos by Ed Wincentsen: Page 123,125,127,133.

Collection of Ed Wincentsen: Page 11,23,25,27,29, 30,31,35,37,39,41,45,49,52,53,63,65,69,74 top,131.

Photos by Jan Chilton: Page 89,101.

Collection of Karen S: Page 112,113,116,117.

Photos by Cindy Bryant: Page 50,51,56,81,85,93, 94,95,103,134,142,143,151,164,165.

Comicbook art by Valerie, Corinna & Marlene: Page 54,55.

Photo Courtsey of Valerie, Corinna & Marlene: Page 105.

Photos by Joanna Parsons: Page 136,138,141.

Photos by Steve & Theresa Clayton: Page 152,153.

# "Who ever thought that Circus Boy would one day become a Monkee?"

# Credits

There are so many people who contributed and helped with this book, and I just want to thank them. If I have missed anybody's name please forgive me, but you know who you are. Thanks for being such a great team!

Susan A. Santo, Nadine, Kirk & Sue White, Birgit, Maggie McManus, Malcolm Searles, Randi L. Waddell, Theresa E. Clayton, Jim Noonan, Caroline Walsh, Charlyne Smith, Lyn Jeffs, Michele Therrien, Cindy Bryant, Vanessa Evans, Mary Klokkert, Lisa Manekofsky, Debbie Sanderson, Maike Ackermann, Frances in the UK, Kelly in Virginia, Sandy Mearing, Tiffany, Sharon in SC, Abby Alterio, Dawn Lively, Daniel Samargis, Sarah, Cassie Sparks, Bob Koenig, Melinda Bruno, Barbara Semans, Cindy in Australia, Shane Worden, Barbara Smith, Debbie Sanderson, Tara L. Harbour, Stephanie Kung, Stephanie Mikhail, Dona McCall, Joanna Parsons, Valerie & her sisters: Marlene & Corinna, Cindy, Kathy Carter, Jan Chilton, Shari Snyder, Cindy Rosecrans, Michelle Evans, Scott Nickerson, Kim Boatman, Mike Gullo, Claire Powell, Gail Friel, Janet Carbert, Shawna Keene, Debbie Prentice, Lynne Barber, Karen S. and Miki.

# Bibliography

(Other good books on the Monkees)

* **MonkeeMania: The True Story of the Monkees**
  Glenn A. Baker
  ISBN: 0-312-00003-0 (pbbk)
  ISBN: 0-85965-256-4 (reprint)

* **The Monkees Tale**
  Eric Lefcowitz
  ISBN: 0-86719-338-7

* **The Monkees Scrapbook**
  Ed Finn & T. Bone
  ISBN: 0-86719-356-5

* **The Monkees Photo Album**
  Joe Russo

* **The Monkees, A Manufactured Image: The Ultimate Reference Guide to Monkee Memories & Memorabilia**
  Edward Reilly, Maggie McManus & William Chadwick
  ISBN: 1-56075-032-4

## Bibliography (cont.)

* **Mutant Monkees**
  Davy Jones & Alan Green
  ISBN: 0-9631235-0-5

* **Hey, Hey We're the Monkees**
  ISBN: 1-57544-012-1

* **I'm A Believer, My Life of Monkees, Music and Madness**
  Micky Dolenz & Mark Bego
  ISBN: 1-56282-847-9

* **They Made A Monkee Out of Me**
  Davy Jones & Alan Green
  ISBN: 0-9618614-0-1

* **Total Control, The Michael Nesmith Story**
  Randi L. Massingill
  ISBN: 0-9658218-3-8

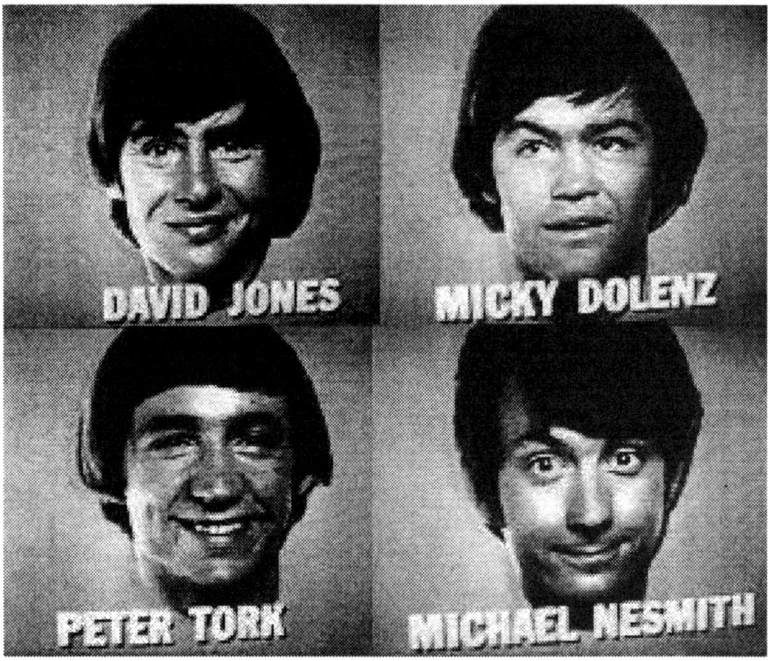
DAVID JONES
MICKY DOLENZ
PETER TORK
MICHAEL NESMITH